WOMAN'S DAY

CRAFTS
for the HOME

WOMAN'S DAY

CRAFTS
for the HOME

BY THE EDITORS OF
WOMAN'S DAY

VIKING STUDIO

VIKING STUDIO
Published by the Penguin Group
Penguin Putnam Inc., 375 Hudson Street,
New York, New York 10014, U.S.A.

Penguin Books Ltd, 27 Wrights Lane, London W8 5TZ, England
Penguin Books Australia Ltd, Ringwood, Victoria, Australia
Penguin Books Canada Ltd, 10 Alcorn Avenue, Toronto, Ontario, Canada M4V 3B2
Penguin Books (N.Z.) Ltd, 182–190 Wairau Road, Auckland 10, New Zealand

Penguin Books Ltd, Registered Offices:
Harmondsworth, Middlesex, England

Woman's Day Staff
EDITOR IN CHIEF: Jane Chesnutt
CRAFTS EDITOR: Cristina Pires Ferreira
WRITER/EDITOR: Nadia Hermos
CAPTIONS: Carol Minkow
COMPUTER ILLUSTRATION: Jason Teig, Wendy Wilson

Research:
Michele Fedele, Sue Kakstys, Dorothy Nocerino

Viking Studio Staff
PROJECT EDITOR: Cyril I. Nelson
BOOK DESIGNER: Kathryn Parise
JACKET DESIGNER: Jaye Zimet

First published in 2000 by Viking Studio, a member of Penguin Putnam Inc.

10 9 8 7 6 5 4 3 2 1

ISBN: 0-670-88782-X

Printed in the United States of America

CONTENTS

INTRODUCTION

At *Woman's Day,* we've long believed that the time and energy spent on a craft project—the imagination and creativity that go into it—are, in a way, as important as the result. Because let's face it: Time is precious these days. Between work and family and everything else, there barely seems to be enough hours in a day to get the "real" stuff done. Taking time to work on a quilt or to paint a decorative vase may seem like a bit of luxury, yet it's an incredibly satisfying effort.

For this, our second *Woman's Day* craft book in four years, we've decided to focus on crafts for the home, on wonderful things for living rooms, bedrooms, kitchens, and even gardens. There are quilts and afghans that are bound to become heirlooms, and projects such as hand-painted picture frames and tableware—delightful to make for yourself or to give as gifts.

The projects are culled from the pages of *Woman's Day* magazine, and no matter what kind of crafts you like, there's plenty here you'll fall in love with. And regardless of your experience as a crafter, we have projects suited to your skills. Whenever possible, we've also given you options and inspirations so you can adapt the projects to your taste and your home's decor—be it country, formal, or modern. Whatever you do, though, don't let our suggestions limit your creative spirit.

We know as well as anyone the pleasure that comes with making something uniquely your own.

I, for one, have a personal fondness for decoupage, and one of my treasures at home is a decoupage plate I made several years ago after *Woman's Day* did a story about the craft. Except for packing up one house and moving to another, my plate has never been out of sight for long. I'm proud to have made it, of course, and must say I did a pretty admirable job for an amateur. But when I look at it, I often think of other things, too—of what I've done in the time since I made the plate, of friends and family who've complimented me on it, even of where that plate and I will be years from now. Making it was a pure and simple pleasure in itself, and having it still gives me another kind of joy. That's exactly what we hope this book brings you.

Jane Chestnutt
EDITOR-IN-CHIEF

A Word from Woman's Day

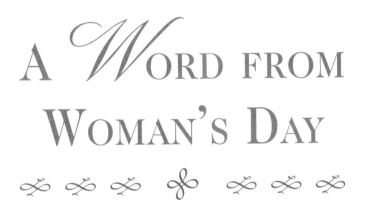

We are proud of this collection selected from the pages of *Woman's Day* magazine, mainly from the nineties. Most are timeless crafts that will look beautiful in your home in the year 2000 and beyond. The designs are varied and fresh and can adapt to any style of decorating—whether sleek and simple or delightfully warm and cluttered. They can be made to blend in with your color scheme or as accents (a bright throw rug on a polished floor, an afghan on a leather couch, a folk art chair on a porch, a flower table in the yard).

Many of the projects can easily be done by beginners with minimal skills in sewing, crochet, woodworking, and painting. Just follow our step-by-step directions and any provided by the product manufacturers.

Feel free to design with available materials. You may not find the exact fabrics we show—although many are classic checks and plaids—and all the afghans are made from basic worsted-weight yarn.

Included are ideas for things you can recycle, especially old chests and chairs. But you can also start with new, inexpensive unfinished furniture, now widely available and a real trend in home decorating because of the many finishes that can be applied. We like the fresh designs on the Little Chests—all the same piece yet adaptable to sten-cil, decoupage, crackle finish, and thumb-tack art.

The quilts are mostly tied comforters that can be stitched up in little time—a day, a weekend, or a few hours a week—because we know how busy you are, and that most stitchers are eager to make a quilt once they get around to it. You can celebrate the seasons with the Autumn Leaves quilt or the Weekend Warmer nine-patch in summery colors (we love the plaid borders), or make a square-patch quickie in Christmas fabrics.

Afghans are no longer just for grannies. The beauties here are dramatic and original and if you make one, no one will accuse you of being dowdy. Crocheters can also whip up a crafty throw rug from scrap (or carefully chosen) fabrics.

We also show you how to paint plain cotton and straw rugs to coordinate with your room.

And for the yard, it's getting hard to resist the amusing ornament tucked into the flower bed or hanging from a tree: a form of celebration of your love of your home.

Then there are the little things, so clever and fetching. You can spend a leisurely afternoon making the decoupaged autumn plate, the handsome twine-and-paper storage boxes, or the little jewel-trimmed mirror.

We know you'll find plenty to enjoy and learn a few new skills at the same time.

Chests and Cabinets

Four top-drawer ways to give a plain chest a charming new look.

Little Chests

❧ ❧ ❧

You can stud it with thumbtacks, stencil it with doilies, antique it with crackle paint, or decoupage it with comics. Do it your way. These four designs were done on unfinished wood chests, but they can be used to revive an old piece, too. You know where it fits in—practically anywhere.

Lace-Stenciled Chest

YOU WILL NEED

- wood stain (we used Anita's Faux Easy Copper)
- large rectangular and round doilies
- spray adhesive or stencil adhesive
- off-white spray paint
- butcher's wax

HOW TO MAKE IT

Note: Before you begin, see *Furniture Preparation*, page 174.

1. Apply stain to the chest and let it dry.

2. To make stencils, cut out the center of a large rectangular doily to use the border on the chest top. Cut large round doilies in half to decorate the drawer fronts. (Use two layers of doily for durability under the paint.)

3. Working outdoors, or in a well-ventilated area, protect the surroundings from overspray with newspapers or a drop cloth. Spray adhesive very lightly on the backs of the doilies and position them on the chest and drawers.

4. Practice spray painting with scrap materials, *following the manufacturer's instructions*. Then spray white paint over the doilies, filling the spaces and lightly surrounding the edges.

5. When the paint is *partially* dry, lift off the doilies and let the lace designs dry completely.

6. Seal the surface with butcher's wax for a lustrous satin finish.

Thumbtack Chest

- ◆ stain (we used Anita's Faux Easy Washed Denim), or acrylic or latex paint for a solidly painted background
- ◆ primer (omit if staining)
- ◆ paintbrushes
- ◆ paper for patterns
- ◆ colored thumbtacks
- ◆ hammer and cloth

HOW TO MAKE IT

Note: Before you begin, see *Furniture Preparation*, page 174.

1. Apply stain, or prime and paint the chest. Let it dry.

2. Cut paper to fit each drawer front and outline a simple design as your pattern. Draw your own design or trace one from a coloring book, calendar, or fabric.

3. Mark dots for tacks about ¾ inch apart along the design outlines.

4. Tape the patterns to the drawers and push the tacks in halfway. Tear away the pattern. You can leave the tacks raised (if they're firmly embedded) or cover a hammer head with cloth and finish sinking them with the hammer.

Comic-Strip Chest

- stain (we used Anita's Faux Easy Poppy Red)
- comic strips or other papers to decoupage
- matte sealer/glue for decoupage
- foam brushes
- brayer or roller (optional)

HOW TO MAKE IT

Note: Before you begin, see *Furniture Preparation*, page 174.

1. Stain the chest and let it dry.

2. Enlarge the comics on a color photocopier and trim them as you like to fit the drawer fronts. Or simply cut a number of strips directly from the comics. (Try out the glue on the paper to make sure the color won't run.)

3. Working on one drawer at a time, brush the sealer/glue on the drawer. When dry, apply a second coat and mount the comic, smoothing it from the center out to remove air bubbles. Use the brayer (roller) for smoothing if you like. Finish off with another coat of sealer/glue and let the glue dry thoroughly.

4. Finally, apply two thin coats of sealer glue as protection, letting each coat dry.

Crackle-Paint Chest

YOU WILL NEED

- white primer
- green or any other color acrylic paint for the undercolor (base coat) to show through the crackled topcoat.
- cream-color (or any other color) acrylic paint for crackled topcoat
- crackle medium
- foam paintbrushes
- clear acrylic finish
- scrap wood or cardboard

HOW TO MAKE IT

Note: Before you begin, see *Furniture Preparation*, page 174.

1. Apply one coat of primer and two coats of undercolor, letting each coat dry. Also paint a board so you can practice the crackling effect later (see step 3).

2. Apply the crackle medium, *following the manufacturer's instructions.*

3. After the medium is dry, and after practicing on your scrap board, brush on the topcoat (cream or any other color) fairly thick to crackle. (Note: Thick paint yields large cracks that show best on furniture, and crackling tends to follow the direction of the strokes: straight strokes give straight cracks, vertical strokes vertical cracks, curved strokes curved cracks.)

4. When the paint is completely dry, apply two coats of clear acrylic finish.

Rose Trellis Cabinet

❧ ❧ ❧

It's practically magical what you can do with the inexpensive, precut sponges by Plaid Enterprises available at crafts stores. The well-shaped stamps have grooves that hold paint for detail lines. You can brush any color you want on the surface. It's just like painting, yet the sponges offer the repetition and technical control of stamping and printing. You can use them on any surface, so even if this cabinet is not for you, try them on something else—glassware, stacked boxes, a storage chest.

YOU WILL NEED

- ◆ an unfinished wood cabinet
- ◆ white semigloss latex paint
- ◆ *Decorator Block Sets* by Plaid Enterprises: Roses 53211, Ivy 53202, and Critters 53222
- ◆ *Decorator Block Glazes:* Ivy Green, New Leaf Green, Sage Green, Baby Pink, Deep Mauve, Burgundy, Lemon, Bark Brown, Bluebell, Black, and Neutral
- ◆ #6 flat and #3 round paintbrushes
- ◆ sponge brush; fine sandpaper
- ◆ slick paper
- ◆ waxed paper or palette
- ◆ colored chalk
- ◆ clear acrylic finish (optional)

This floral beauty looks hand painted, but it's printed with special stamps that create realistic effects.

Note: Before you begin, see *Furniture Preparation*, page 174.

1. Brush a base coat of white paint on the cabinet and let it dry. Rub the paint with sandpaper, following the wood grain. Dust off the residue with a tack cloth.

2. Paint one or two more coats of white, letting each coat dry, and sand between each coat. Let the paint dry for 24 hours.

3. Practice sponge printing: Read the block-kit directions; they are fully detailed. Since the cabinet has a slick paint surface, practice printing on shiny paper without sliding the block. To begin, brush paint on the bottom of the sponge block, press the block gently onto the surface, and lift. Print two or three impressions from one paint application; the lighter prints will create depth and variation in the design.

4. Make chalk lines to indicate the flow of a floral design on the cabinet front and doorframe. Or plan a detailed design on paper and trace the shapes lightly on the cabinet using transfer paper. Best of all, work freehand and improvise as you go. If you make a mistake, you can wipe off the wet paint with a damp towel and start over. Some general guidelines follow.

Large pink roses: Brush Pink and Mauve glaze on the large rose sponge block; add some shading with Burgundy. Scatter prints on the cabinet within your design framework, overlapping some side by side. Reload the sponge block and repeat as necessary.

Large yellow roses: Clean the block and reload it with Lemon glaze. Tip the edges and center with Burgundy blended in. Scatter prints within the design as before.

Buds: Use Pink and Mauve as for the large pink roses, adding green for the leaves on large and small buds. Repeat with the Lemon and Burgundy combination of the yellow roses.

Leaves: Load the sponge block for the large rose leaf with Ivy Green, New Leaf, and/or Sage. Edge some leaves with Burgundy. Fill in the spaces among the flowers with leaves. Print the smaller rose leaves in the same way, leaving room for a few ivy leaves.

Ivy: Use Ivy Green, Sage, and a little New Leaf glaze, alternating the main color on different-size leaves. Print ivy descending on the left side of the cabinet, and a short strand extending from the back left corner on the cabinet top. Use pale third or fourth presses to fill in open areas around the trellis.

Butterfly: Paint Black on the body and Pink, Burgundy, and Yellow on the wings. Print butterflies among the flowers, one on the right front and another on the left near the ivy. With the round brush, give them Black antennae.

Bluebird: Use Bluebell for wings, upper body, and head; Bark Brown for the chest; and Black for the beak and eye. Print 2 birds on the front at the edge of masses of flowers or leaves.

Vines: Following vining instructions in the kit, use the round brush and Neutral, Brown, and Ivy Green glazes to connect flowers and leaves with brown stems and green vines. Keep the color pale, allowing a few dark edges, created by the brush as you draw the lines.

5. Cabinet trim: With the flat brush and Bluebell glaze mixed with two or three drops of water, paint the molding under the cabinet top. Blot the wet paint with a damp paper towel to mottle the color. Let the paint dry for 48 hours.

6. Apply a clear acrylic finish if the cabinet will be used heavily.

Crackle-Finish Dresser

❧ ❧ ❧

The moldings are optional additions to this piece, but they help to accent and organize the shape. Include them if you can, or paint existing trims on the chest in contrasting colors. Miniature saw-and-miter box sets, available in crafts stores, can be used to cut the corners for the moldings.

YOU WILL NEED

- an old or unfinished chest
- wood putty
- sandpaper
- red (or any other color) flat latex or acrylic paint for undercoat and trims
- cream (or any other color) latex or acrylic paint for topcoat
- crackle medium
- paintbrushes
- ½-inch-wide half-round wood molding of desired length (optional); see Step 5
- saw, miter box, wood glue, and brads for molding
- clear acrylic finish

Note: Test each step on scrap wood, or cardboard, or on the back of the chest to try out colors and crackling techniques before painting.

HOW TO MAKE IT

Note: Before you begin, see *Furniture Preparation*, page 174.

1. Apply primer and let it dry. Sand lightly.

2. Paint the dresser red, letting each coat dry.

3. *Following the manufacturer's instructions*, apply a coat of crackle medium to the entire chest or wherever you want a crackled surface. (We left the feet, front edge of the top, and red trim smooth.)

4. Apply cream color (or any other surface color) to crackle. Note that the paint will crack in the direction of the strokes; thick paint makes larger cracks, which are appropriate on furniture.

5. To trim the drawers, paint strips of ½-inch half-round molding red. Measure where you want them on the drawer fronts about ½ inch in from the sides and cut the strips to fit, mitering the corners. Glue and nail the moldings in place.

6. Spray paint new metal pulls and reattach.

7. Apply the clear acrylic finish.

> This is a handsome easy finish for an old chest that will look good in any room in the house. The contrasting trims add character.

Floral Decoupage Chest

❧ ❧ ❧

Floral cutouts from books and other publications are easy to apply to create the relaxed mood of provincial furniture. The textured background is applied with irregular brush-work (scumbling) and ordinary latex paints.

Note: Before you begin, see *Furniture Preparation*, page 174.

1. Brush on the primer and let it dry.

2. Apply two coats of white paint and let each coat dry.

3. With the artist's brush, work the lighter green over the white by scrubbing on small amounts of paint every which way to create a textured look. Let the light coat dry.

4. With the dampened natural sponge, apply a film of the darker green. Use the dampened scrubber to blend in and wipe off the wet paint, removing some of the undercolor as well. Let the dark coat dry.

5. Position paper or fabric cutouts on the chest and drawer fronts wherever you want to add emphasis or interest. Tape the pieces in place and lightly outline the placement with a pencil.

6. Remove a few cutouts at a time. Apply decoupage sealer/glue in position on the chest and smooth on the pieces, pressing from the centers out to eliminate air bubbles. Apply a finishing coat of sealer/glue and let it dry.

7. Apply the water-base finish. When it's dry, replace the hardware.

YOU WILL NEED

- an old or unfinished chest
- primer (for glossy surfaces if painting an old chest)
- linen white and 2 shades of green eggshell-finish latex paint
- 1- to 2-inch flat paintbrushes, including an artist's or utility bristle brush
- natural sponge
- household scrubber sponge
- floral cutouts from fabric or paper
- matte decoupage sealer/glue
- low-luster water-base finish
- sandpaper
- tack cloth

*I*t's a rare home that doesn't have the perfect niche for a useful little chest like this one. Cool green paint and a scattering of decoupage flowers will give an old chest a new lease on life.

Stenciled Blanket Chest

❧ ❧ ❧

Chests like these are indispensable for storage, and you can sit on them or pile things on top. Line the inside with adhesive wall covering or cedar paper to keep stored materials from discoloring or insect damage.

YOU WILL NEED

- unfinished wooden chest (large toy chest or blanket chest)
- white acrylic primer
- off-white flat latex paint
- yellow-ocher flat latex or 8-ounce jar of acrylic paint
- red and green acrylic paints (Liquitex Napthol Crimson and Chrome Oxide Green)
- waxed stencil paper
- X-Acto knife
- one or two ½-inch stencil brushes
- fine sandpaper
- two 2-inch flat paintbrushes

*T*he influence of Pennsylvania Dutch folk art is unmistakable in the stylized flower designs on this chest.

- clear satin water-base or polyurethane finish
- painter's tape or masking tape
- palette or coated paper plate

HOW TO MAKE IT

Note: Before you begin, see *Furniture Preparation*, page 174.

1. Apply one coat of white primer and two coats of white paint to the outside of the chest, letting each coat dry. Sand lightly between coats.

2. Pencil a 5½-inch-wide band about 2¾ inches in from each end of the lid and down the front of the chest. Mask the outer edges of the bands with tape, pressing the tape firmly down. Paint the bands yellow. Remove the tape. Let the paint dry.

3. Tape the stencil paper over the pattern, page 14, and trace red flowers on one stencil. Trace green leaves and stems on another, including a few lines from the flowers as guidelines for placement (see *Stenciling Basics*, page 177). Trace five border crescents on a third stencil.

4. Cut out the stencil shapes with the X-Acto knife, leaving the background intact.

5. Using the stencil as a pattern, trace three flowers on each yellow lid band, ending the middle flowers at the broken line to fit and flopping the stencil so that the flowers on the right band face right and those on the left band face left. Trace flowers on the chest front as shown, and trace two, centered 1 inch apart, on each end.

6. Tape the stencil to the chest to paint the red parts first. Stipple the paint in from the edges and leave the centers lighter to shade the shapes. Remove the stencil.

7. Clean the stencil with soap and water before the paint dries or let the paint dry hard, so you can flop the stencil to paint the reversed flowers.

8. Stencil the green parts.

9. Lightly brush green on the centers of the flowers. When the paint is dry, stamp red dots in the centers with a pencil eraser.

10. Stencil crescent borders next to the bands.

11. Optional: Draw and cut a stencil for the name of the owner or a special date and paint it on the center of the top of the lid. Alphabet stencils are available in art supply and crafts stores.

Plan your stencil by tracing the letters you need evenly spaced on graph paper. Then trace the entire stencil onto stencil paper and cut it out.

12. Apply two coats of finish over the chest.

X - stamp dots with eraser; do not cut out

Border

end middle flowers on lid bands

BLANKET CHEST STENCIL PATTERN

Striped Cabinet

❧ ❧ ❧

If the soft pastels of the country don't go with your themes, a striped cabinet like this can be done in dark colors for a home office or bright ones to hold tapes in a child's room. The tender vines can be transformed into any stenciled or stamped images. It's adaptable.

YOU WILL NEED

- an unfinished or old cabinet
- acrylic paints (white and soft green or any other color)
- two 2-inch and one 1-inch foam brushes
- liner brush
- round brush
- fine sandpaper (on block, optional)
- tack cloth
- ruler
- light pencil
- white plastic eraser
- optional: stencil or sponge stamps for vines or other motifs
- clear acrylic finish

So you're no Rembrandt? Then stripes are a good bet for making an unfinished cabinet look as if it had been painted by a pro.

15 ❧

Note: Before you begin, see *Furniture Preparation*, page 174.

1. Mix a stain of approximately 2 parts white acrylic paint to 2 parts water. (Test it on the back of the cabinet or on scrap wood. One coat, when dry, should let the wood show through slightly. Add more paint or water if needed.) Brush the stain on the cabinet, door, and drawer. When it's dry, sand the surfaces lightly.

2. With the pencil and ruler, lightly mark guidelines for stripes 1 inch apart across the cabinet top and around the sides.

3. Paint every other space green (or another contrasting color), using the 1-inch-wide brush freehand. Let dry.

4. With the liner brush, paint a fine stripe between each pair of wide stripes.

5. Paint the doorframe and stripes, as shown in the photograph.

6. Paint the vines freehand with the round brush or make a pattern by tracing the design, opposite, then scribbling on the back of the design with a soft pencil. Place the pattern face up on the chest and go over the lines with pencil to transfer the design. Repeat to lengthen it, connecting the lines. Then paint following the lines and shading as in the photograph. (Or, instead of the vines, apply other designs with stencils or stamps.) Let the paint dry.

7. Erase visible pencil lines and sand the surface very lightly. Then apply the finish, *following the manufacturer's instructions.*

STRIPED CABINET

Plaid-Painted Dresser

❧ ❧ ❧

You can paint this freehand on an old dresser or a new, unfinished one. The size of the foam brush establishes the width of the stripes and one color, mixed in various proportions with white, creates the three shades for the plaid.

For its smart good looks, plaid is a winner on this eye-catching chest.

YOU WILL NEED

- ◆ white primer
- ◆ a dark-color enamel paint (Red Devil duratex colors Midnight Blue)
- ◆ flat white latex paint
- ◆ two 2¾-inch and one 1-inch foam brushes
- ◆ 2 pans, cans, or jars and sticks for mixing colors

- scrap wood or cardboard
- masking or painter's tape
- kitchen plastic wrap
- clear finish
- brass drawer pulls (optional)

HOW TO MAKE IT

Note: Before you begin, see *Furniture Preparation*, page 174.

1. Brush on a coat of white primer with one large foam brush. Let the primer dry.

2. Mix a dark-color enamel paint and flat white latex paint about half and half to make a medium shade for the background. Mix a slightly darker shade for the stripes and a slightly lighter shade for the top of the chest. (Test your colors on scrap wood or cardboard or the back of the dresser and let them dry. Then look at them, preferably where the dresser will be placed, to judge the colors.) Mix enough paint to work each section and keep the paint covered with plastic wrap when not in use.

3. With the other large foam brush, paint two coats of the background color on the dresser and the drawer fronts, letting each coat dry.

4. Protect the edge of the previous paint with masking tape as needed and paint the lightest color on the top of the dresser.

5. Lightly pencil the placement of 1-inch-wide vertical stripes evenly spaced about 2 inches apart on the drawer fronts, starting at the centers and ending with a stripe at each side. Then indicate horizontal across the top, bottom, and center of each drawer.

6. With a 1-inch foam brush and the darker mixed color, paint the vertical stripes freehand. When the stripes are dry, paint the horizontal stripes. Let the paint dry.

7. With the 1-inch brush, stroke the unmixed paint color full strength over the junctures of the stripes to form the dark squares. Let the paint dry thoroughly.

8. Apply two coats of finish, letting each coat dry.

9. Attach new brass drawer pulls.

❧❧❧ ✦ ❧❧❧

TABLES

—❧—

❧❧❧ ✦ ❧❧❧

Could there be any more natural motif than leaves to bring out the beauty of wood?

Autumn Leaves Table

❧ ❧ ❧

Three different wood-color stains give the rich tones to this table. The three-toned theme could be used with equally good results on other furniture. The wooden glued-on leaves are optional.

YOU WILL NEED

- an unfinished wooden table (the one illustrated is a side table 14 inches wide × 28 inches long × 28 inches high)
- three different-color wood stains (Minwax Wood Finish Red Mahogany 225, Special Walnut 224, and Cherry 235)
- natural stain (Minwax Woodsheen Natural 705)
- clear polyurethane or other protective finish
- mineral spirits (for cleanup)
- small round paintbrush
- clean, soft, lint-free cloths or foam brushes
- craft knife
- self-adhesive shelving plastic (such as Con-Tact)
- tack cloth
- fine sandpaper
- tracing paper
- masking tape
- ¼-inch smooth plywood and saber saw with narrow blade for the glued-on wooden leaves

Note: If your table comes unassembled, stain the pieces before putting them together.

HOW TO MAKE IT

Note: Before you begin, see *Furniture Preparation*, page 174.

1. Trace the three leaf patterns printed on page 22. Cut out the patterns and outline 14 assorted leaves (or enough for a table border) on the back of the adhesive plastic. Cut out the plastic shapes.

2. Arrange the cutouts on the tabletop, trace the positions lightly, then peel off the paper backing and adhere the cutouts firmly in place.

3. Brush on mahogany stain and quickly wipe off any excess with a cloth or sponge. Remove the cutouts and let the stain dry.

4. Mask the frame (or apron) next to the legs of an assembled table with tape. Stain the legs walnut and again wipe off excess stain. Let the stain dry and remove the tape.

5. Mask the legs if necessary and stain the frame Cherry.

6. Outline the leaves and veins freehand with the round brush and walnut stain (practice drawing with the brush on scrap wood). Let the lines dry thoroughly.

7. Apply natural stain on the tabletop only. Let the stain dry. Put the table together now, if it is not assembled.

8. Wooden leaves: Trace assorted leaves from the patterns onto plywood. Cut them out with the saber saw (see *Making Wooden Cutouts*, page 176). Sand the edges. Give the leaves a light coat of walnut stain. When dry, add darker walnut veins with the round brush. Glue the leaves evenly spaced along the table frame.

9. Apply two coats of clear finish, letting each coat dry.

AUTUMN LEAVES TABLE PATTERNS

- a small table
- broken crockery and/or ceramic tiles
- grout
- tile glue or glue gun
- latex semigloss paint and primer or another finish for the wood
- paintbrushes
- household sponge or rags
- rubber gloves
- sandpaper
- optional: marbles and glue gun (or lattice strips or ½-inch quarter-round molding, miter box, and brads to edge a rectangular table)

*H*ate to sand and stain? Turn scruffy old tabletops into an enchanting shimmer of color and glass.

Crockery and Glass Table

❧ ❧ ❧

You can use an eye-catching side table like this one just about anywhere. Have a good time breaking up chipped dishes, or use sea glass or tiles, and glue the pieces to the tabletop. Then fill in the spaces with tile grout and you'll have a marvelous unique piece.

HOW TO MAKE IT

1. Place the crockery in a cloth and break it with a hammer into approximately 1- to 2-inch pieces. If larger pieces have pretty designs or textures, they can be used as focal points in the design.

2. Wash and dry the table. Sand the surface lightly. If the table is rectangular, you can glue and nail lattice or molding strips around the edge to form a rim (cut mitered corners on the molding). Lattice can be placed against the edge. Molding should be placed along the top, flush at the outside.

3. Arrange the crockery shards on the top of the table close together, about ⅛ inch to ½ inch apart. Attach the shards to the wood with tile glue or hot glue. Let the glue set.

4. *Following the manufacturer's instructions*, mix the grout and spread it over and between the crockery, smoothing it with your fingers (wear rubber gloves) and a damp sponge or rag. Finish the edge of the round table smoothly. Wipe the grout off the exposed exterior wood.

5. Let the grout dry, then clean the surfaces as directed. Add another layer of grout if you want to make the surface more even.

6. Paint the rest of the table. Glue on marbles or glue and grout chips along unfinished edges.

Coffee Table with Magazine Shelf

❧ ❧ ❧

This table with its useful shelf is not hard to build. You may be able to have the pieces precut at a lumberyard; all are straight cuts. If you're an experienced woodworker, you can adapt the basic design to almost any size or height.

SIZE

24 inches wide × 36 inches long × 17½ inches high

YOU WILL NEED

- ½ sheet of ½-inch-thick smooth plywood
- two 16-inch and one 28-inch length of 1 × 4 pine for frame
- four 17-inch lengths of 2 × 2 for legs
- 15 each 2-inch 16-gauge wood screws and ⅜-inch button wood plugs
- ten 1½-inch finishing nails
- nail set
- 13 feet of ½-inch iron-on veneer
- latex or acrylic paint
- water-base or polyurethane clear finish
- drill with ⅛-inch and ⅜-inch bits
- wood glue
- natural wood filler
- fine sandpaper
- tack cloth
- paintbrushes
- iron
- craft knife
- bar clamps or masking tape

*W*hen it's time for a snack, just slip the coffee-table books and magazines off the top of the table into the handy shelf below.

1. With the smoother side of the plywood face up, cut the tabletop 24 × 36 inches and the shelf 17½ × 28 inches.

2. *Following the manufacturer's instructions*, iron the veneer to the edges of the tabletop and to one long edge (this will be the open edge) of the shelf.

3. To frame the shelf, follow Diagram 1, at right. Glue and nail the 28-inch 1 × 4 against the back edge of the shelf, flush along the bottom. Leaving the back corners of the frame open, nail a 16-inch 1 × 4 along each side of the shelf. The side frames will end 1½ inches from the front corners (see Diagram 1). Sink the nailheads below the surface by placing the nail set over each one and tapping it with a hammer. Wipe off any excess glue with a damp cloth.

4. With the frame upside down, glue the legs into the corners; tape or clamp them until the glue sets (Diagram 2). To leave space for centered screws through the top of the legs, predrill off-center holes for screws with the ⅛-inch bit through the sides of legs into the ends of the frame (insert two through the back legs from the back and one from the side, and two through the front legs from the front). Drill space for ⅜-inch plug at the top of each screw hole. Insert the screws, adding a bead of glue on each joint before you tighten the screw.

5. Place the tabletop facedown on a drop cloth or newspapers. Center the assembled frame upside down on top and measure and mark the placement. Nail part way through diagonally opposite legs to hold the frame in place temporarily. Stand the table up. Mark the leg positions on the top and drill holes for a countersunk, capped screw through the top into the center of each leg. Remove the temporary nails with a hammer claw.

6. Glue and screw the top to the frame.

7. Put a drop of glue in each screw hole and insert a plug. Cover nail holes with filler.

8. Sand the wood lightly, following the grain and rounding the edges. Dust with the tack cloth.

9. Paint or stain the table as you like or color-stain as follows: Thin the paint with approxi-mately an equal amount of water. With a damp-ened sponge or a brush, test a swatch for coverage on the underside of the table or on scrap wood. Let the test dry, then adjust the proportions if necessary. Stain the table. If you can't reach in-side to paint the shelf, attach the brush or sponge firmly to a paint stick or dowel. Let the paint dry. Sand the surface lightly if the wood grain is raised.

10. *Following the manufacturer's instructions*, ap-ply a clear finish in thin coats to make a lustrous surface, sanding lightly between coats.

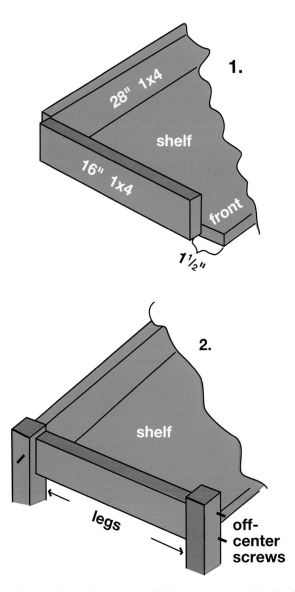

COFFEE TABLE WITH MAGAZINE SHELF

Pastel Table/Bench

✤ ✤ ✤

*E*ven in the smallest spaces you'll have a place to put the fruit bowl, drinks, and magazines with this slim table that doubles as a bench.

Practical in any room, this table/bench is easy to make, if you can cut wood and drill holes. The scroll brackets in the front are purchased and decorative, therefore they are optional, not structural.

SIZE

36 inches long × 12 inches wide × 16¾ inches high

YOU WILL NEED

- ¾-inch birch or other smooth plywood for top and legs
- two 36-inch lengths of 1 × 4 pine
- optional: two ¾ × 7 × 7-inch decorative brackets (we used Quarter Circle Brackets 104 from Vintage Wood Works, 513 South Adams #1819, Fredericksburg, TX 78624; 512-997-9513)
- 1¼-inch finishing nails
- 1¼-inch No. 9 or 10 flathead wood screws

- ⅜-inch-diameter wood plugs (8 button plugs and 10 flat) or natural wood filler
- wood glue
- medium and fine sandpaper
- tack cloth
- two 12-inch-span clamps
- ⅜-inch-diameter countersink screw drill or equivalent
- acrylic paint and a semigloss water-base or polyurethane clear finish

HOW TO MAKE IT

1. Cut the wood (except the brackets) to the sizes and shapes shown on the Assembly Diagram, below. See *Making Wooden Cutouts*, page 176.

2. Clamp the legs between the rails, ½ inch in from the ends of the rails. Check to make sure the top is level and the legs are stable. Drill countersunk holes for 2 screws at each juncture through the rails into the legs. Glue and screw

the rails to the legs. Glue button plugs into the holes (or cover the holes with filler when the assembly is completed).

3. Glue the brackets under the corners formed on the front of the frame. Set a nail at each end of each bracket into the rails and legs.

4. Center the assembled frame upside down on the tabletop and mark the outline. Then stand up the frame with the top over it within the marks. Mark the placement and drill countersunk pilot holes for five evenly spaced screws through the top into each rail. Glue and screw the top to the frame. Glue flat plugs into the holes or use wood filler.

5. Sand the wood edges and filler smooth, rounding the corners. Dust off the residue with the tack cloth.

6. Thin one part acrylic paint with one part water to make a color stain (or use paint full strength, if you prefer). Then brush on the stain in the direction of the wood grain and let it dry.

7. Apply two coats of protective finish, *following the manufacturer's instructions*.

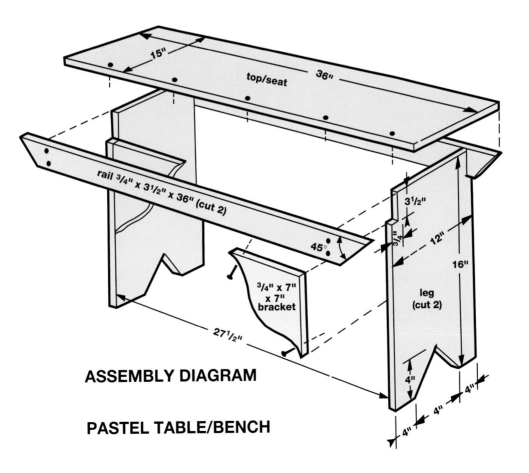

ASSEMBLY DIAGRAM

PASTEL TABLE/BENCH

Vinegar-Painted Table

❧ ❧ ❧

An updated version of a colonial painting technique, you can use vinegar painting to decorate any wood furniture. Paint the undercolor in enamel, then apply a vinegar paint you mix from dry pigments (which give the intense colors). Dab or scrape off the wet topping to create the textures. For the table use crumpled plastic wrap, a graining tool, and thumbprints.

YOU WILL NEED

- ◆ an unfinished or old wood table
- ◆ semigloss white oil-base enamel for the undercoat
- ◆ Crayola Powdered Paint in red and green (or any other colors)
- ◆ 32-ounce bottle of white vinegar
- ◆ 1-pound box of granulated sugar
- ◆ one small bottle of liquid detergent
- ◆ foam paintbrushes
- ◆ plastic wrap
- ◆ graining tool (from a paint store) or a comb
- ◆ fine sandpaper
- ◆ tack cloth
- ◆ scrap wood or cardboard to sample colors and practice techniques

Vinegar painting is not only unique and dazzling, it's fun to do.

- gloss or satin polyurethane finish (do not use a water-base finish)
- 2-cup jars and plastic spoons for mixing
- glass measuring cup
- measuring spoons

HOW TO MAKE IT

Note: Before you begin, see *Furniture Preparation*, page 174.

1. Apply two coats of enamel as the base color, letting each coat dry thoroughly. Paint the sample board as well.

2. *To make vinegar paint:* Put 2 tablespoons of powdered color into the 2-cup jar. Into the measuring cup pour ½ cup of vinegar, 1 teaspoon sugar, and a squirt of detergent. Slowly stir the vinegar mixture into the dry color until it assumes the consistency of heavy cream. (A dab on paper held vertically should not run.) Add dry color to thicken the paint or vinegar mixture to thin it. Mix 2 cups of paint (four times the test amount) for a large piece of furniture.

3. Brush the vinegar paint over the enamel on the scrap board. While it's wet, practice dabbing it with crumpled plastic wrap, scratching paint off with a graining tool or comb, and making designs with thumbprints. It is important to monitor the drying time so you can plan to apply paint in workable sections to the furniture.

GRAINING

4. Now apply the vinegar paint over the enamel on the furniture and make the designs and textures as you go. Don't worry about mistakes—wet or dry, the vinegar paint can be wiped off with a damp sponge or paper towel.

DABBING

5. When the paint is completely dry, protect it with two coats of polyurethane, letting each coat dry thoroughly.

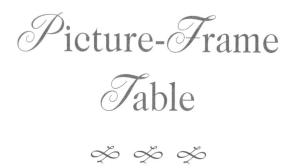

Picture-Frame Table

❦ ❦ ❦

Pretty as a picture, this eye-catching side table is assembled with glue and screws, then painted, and finished with the image of your choice placed under the glass.

YOU WILL NEED

- 14 × 17-inch flat, 2-inch-wide wooden picture frame (or any other adequate size for the tabletop) with glass and backing
- picture
- mat or ribbon used as a mat
- four 16-inch wood 2 × 2 strips for legs
- eight 16-gauge 2-inch flathead wood screws
- eight ⅜-inch flat wooden plugs
- white acrylic paint or desired finish
- 1-inch flat paintbrush
- water-base or polyurethane clear finish
- wood glue
- drill with ³⁄₁₆-inch and ⅜-inch bits
- duct tape or brads

HOW TO MAKE IT

1. Remove the backing and glass from the frame. Trace the top of the table legs about ⅛ inch in from the corners on the underside and on the top.

2. Firmly hold the leg in place under the frame (or ask someone to hold it). With the ⅛-inch bit, drill two pilot holes through the top for screws at least ¾ inch apart in the marked space at each corner and into the top of the leg. With the ⅜-inch bit, drill space at the top of each hole for the plugs.

3. Screw the legs in place. Glue the plugs into the holes.

4. Stain the frame and legs with one coat of acrylic paint thinned with an equal amount of water, or paint or stain as you like.

5. When the stain is dry, apply two coats of clear finish, letting each coat dry.

6. Turn the table over onto a flat cloth-covered surface. Insert the glass and make sure it's lint free. Then insert the mat and the picture. (Or glue ribbon around the picture, instead of using a mat.) Install the backing with strong tape (duct tape) or brace it firmly with brads hammered into the side of the frame.

A charming side table is a breeze to make from a ready-made wooden frame with glass and precut legs.

- old or new table
- decorator sponge blocks and glazes by Plaid Enterprises (we used Trumpet Flowers)
- white primer
- light shade of flat latex enamel or acrylic paint
- clear water-base or polyurethane finish
- flat paintbrush

Note: Before you begin, see *Furniture Preparation*, page 174.

1. Apply a coat of white primer, then two coats of a light shade of flat latex enamel or acrylic paint, letting each coat dry.

2. Stamp flowers and foliage with sponge blocks and glazes. Full directions for use are included with the blocks and glazes.

3. When the paint is thoroughly dry, protect the surface with the clear finish, *following the manufacturer's directions.*

Town and Country Table

❧ ❧ ❧

Old tables like this may be plentiful in attics and garage sales, but they are often rickety. To repair small dents in the surface, cover the damaged wood with a few layers of clean, moist cotton cloth and briefly apply a hot iron. To firm up loose joints, separate them and scrape off the old glue, wind thread on the tenon (protruding member), then glue the joint back together.

Outdoor Flower Table

❧ ❧ ❧

Picture several different flower-shaped tables, one next to each chair in the garden. Make them bright and whimsical, and establish a place for each one, so you don't poke too many holes in your lawn.

YOU WILL NEED

- 20-inch square of ½-inch plywood
- 24-inch (or longer) × 1-inch-diameter dowel for leg
- 1½-inch 16-gauge screw to attach leg
- 1½-inch finishing nail
- white primer
- acrylic paints (FolkArt School Bus Yellow, Poppy Red, Autumn Leaves, and Fresh Foliage)
- wood putty
- nail set
- medium and fine sandpaper
- tack cloth
- wood glue
- drill
- foam or bristle paintbrushes
- clear satin polyurethane or exterior finish
- mineral spirits for polyurethane cleanup
- saber saw

What could be handier or more cheerful out of doors that this pretty chair-side flower table that you can stick into the ground wherever it's needed.

HOW TO MAKE IT

1. Enlarge the flower pattern, page 34, directly on the wood (draw a 10 by 10 grid of 2-inch squares on the wood first) or on paper (see *How to Enlarge Patterns*, page 174). Cut the flower from

wood for the tabletop (see *Making Wooden Cutouts*, page 176).

2. With the saw and/or a knife, cut a centered point at one end of the dowel for the table leg.

3. In the center of the table, drill a pilot hole for the countersunk screw. When the drill bit protrudes, center the flat end of the leg over the bit and continue the hole into the center of the leg.

4. Glue and screw the leg in place. Add a finishing nail through the dowel into the tabletop to keep the leg from spinning on the screw. Sink the nailhead by placing a nail set over the nailhead and tapping it with a hammer.

5. Fill the holes and edges (if necessary) with putty. Let the putty dry. Sand the edges and putty.

6. Apply a coat of primer and let it dry.

7. Paint the flower yellow and the leg green. When the paint is dry, paint the flower center as shown on the pattern and in the photograph.

8. Apply two coats of finish, letting each coat dry.

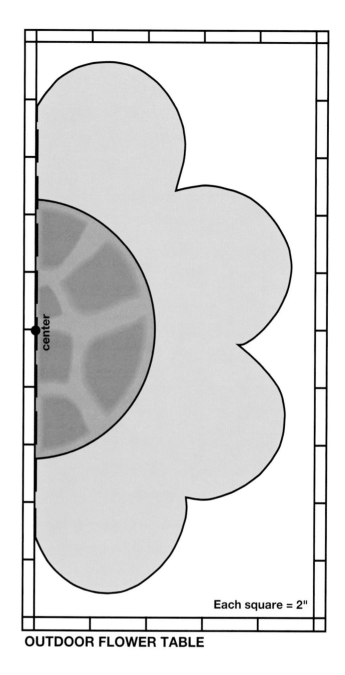

center

Each square = 2"

OUTDOOR FLOWER TABLE

Tile-Topped Table

✎ ✎ ✎

A top of bright ceramic tile can turn any old table into a great indoor or outdoor server.

Classic and enduring, tiles are easy to care for, and colors in bright or earth tones generally just hit the spot. Find local sources in your telephone directory. And if you don't have a miter box for the moldings, look for small saws and miter boxes in crafts stores.

- an old or unfinished rectangular or square wood table
- tiles approximately 4 inches square or other size to fit the top evenly spaced ⅛ to ½ inch apart
- tile glue or any strong adhesive
- grout
- ½-inch quarter-round molding for edges
- small saw and miter box
- wood glue
- 1-inch brads
- sandpaper
- sponge
- wood putty
- putty knife or spatula
- primer
- interior or exterior paint
- paintbrushes

1. Wash, dry, and lightly sand the table.

2. Cut the molding with 45-degree mitered corners to fit along the tabletop top flush at the outer edges. Glue the molding to the top with wood glue, then nail with brads. Fill any cracks with putty and let it dry. Sand the putty smooth.

3. Arrange the tiles and glue them in place.

4. When the glue has dried, spread grout between the tiles with the putty knife, *following the grout manufacturer's directions.* Wipe the haze from the top with the sponge, again following the manufacturer's directions.

5. Prime, then paint the wood surfaces.

Quilts and Afghans

Cozy Country Quilt

✥ ✥ ✥

The blocks are made from long strips of fabric, sewn together and cut into squares. The striped border is made from leftovers. You can have fun with this pattern by playing with color schemes. It's all straight stitching and easily quilted with two borders of machine stitching and a few ties.

SIZES

Twin: 66 × 96 inches; full: 78 × 96 inches; queen: 84 × 108 inches; king: 108 × 120 inches

YOU WILL NEED

- for the top, four 44-inch-wide cotton or cotton-blend fabrics (avoid stripes), each fabric: 2¾ yards (twin), 2¾ yards (full), 3⅛ yards (queen), and 3½ yards (king)
- for the backing, use a full-size sheet for the twin- and full-size quilts, a king-size sheet for the queen-size quilt; and 2 queen-size sheets for the king-size quilt
- white or matching cotton thread
- quilt batting

Make this quilt in the early fall so you and your brood can cuddle up when the weather turns frightful. It's an ample bedspread, too.

- 2 skeins of DMC floss or pearl cotton and an embroidery needle for ties
- rotary cutter, mat, and see-through ruler (optional)

HOW TO MAKE IT

Note: Before you begin, see *Quilting Basics*, page 176.

1. From the full length of each fabric cut 2-inch-wide strips (fold fabric to cut through several layers at once): 6 strips for the twin, 8 strips for the full, 9 strips for the queen, and 12 strips for the king. Label the colors A, B, C, and D in the order that you want to assemble them. (They can be graded dark to light or arranged with accent colors in the centers, as in the photograph.) Then stack the strips in order in piles of one of each color.

2. Cut four 3½-inch-wide strips lengthwise from each of three fabrics you choose for solid-color borders; label these 1, 3, and 4 and set them aside. (Border 2 is pieced from stripes of all four colors.)

3. Stitch the 2-inch-wide strips together in order A, B, C, D to have 6 striped panels for twin size, 8 for full, 9 for queen, and 12 for king.

4. Cut across the panels every 6½ inches to have 6½-inch-square blocks: 84 for twin, 108 for full, 140 for queen, and 224 for king. Save any leftovers for border 2.

5. Stitch the blocks into strips, alternating the direction of the stripes, as follows: Start the first strip with the block upright and color A at the left. Add the second block next to it with color A at the top (see diagram for Strip 1, page 40). Alternate this pattern until you have a strip of 7 blocks for twin size, 9 for full, 10 for queen, and 14 for king.

6. Start the second strip with color A at the top and alternate the blocks as before (see diagram for Strip 2). Be sure to keep the same seam allowance so that the block seams will match. It's a good idea to check often against the previous strip.

7. Stitch the third strip and all odd-numbered strips the same way as the first, and even-numbered strips the same way as the second, to have a total of 12 strips for twin size, 12 for full, 14 for queen, and 16 for king.

8. Stitch strip *2* below strip *1* and alternate strips in this manner to form the patchwork.

9. *Border 1:* Stitch a strip of the fabric you've cut for border 1 to each long side of the patchwork. Trim the ends even with the patchwork. Add border 1 to the top and bottom of the patchwork, including the ends of the side borders. Trim the ends even with the previous borders.

10. *Border 2:* Cut 2½-inch-wide strips lengthwise from the excess of the four fabrics. Stitch these together in panels as you did for the blocks. Then cut across the panels every 3½ inches. Stitch the strips together to make borders long enough for the edges. Stitch borders to the sides, then to the top and bottom of border 1.

11. Add borders 3 and 4.

12. Undo the hem from the backing sheet and press the sheet flat. (For the king-size quilt, then stitch the two sheets together.) Lay out the sheet right side up. Place the patchwork facedown on top of the sheet. Pin the edges firmly together and trim the sheet to match the patchwork.

13. Stitch along the sides and top, leaving the bottom open. Smooth the batting on top. Holding the corners, roll the layers together from the top toward the bottom opening, turn the quilt inside out, and shake the batting to even it out inside.

14. Turn in the bottom edges and slipstitch the bottom closed. Then topstitch ⅜ inch from the edges through all thicknesses to secure the batting. Then stitch along the seam between borders 1 and 2.

15. *Ties:* Insert a pin through all layers at the corners of each square next to border 1. At each pin, with needle and floss take a stitch from front to back and up to front again. Tie ends in a square knot and trim them to ½ inch. Add ties to the patchwork field if you like.

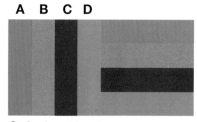

Strip 1 – repeat

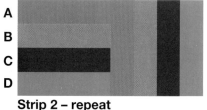

Strip 2 – repeat

Repeat Strips 1 and 2 as directed.

COZY COUNTRY QUILT

"Patriotic" Quilt

❦ ❦ ❦

Although it looks complex, this handsome bed-cover is a simple arrangement of squares and strips in varied patterns, all cut and stitched with straight lines. And it's tied, not quilted. The art is in arranging prints in varied shades of red and blue (or other colors of your choice) to achieve a rich allover effect.

SIZE

74 × 94 inches for a twin-, full- or queen-size bed.

YOU WILL NEED

Note: Letters following the fabric yardage refer to the center (A) and borders of the quilt on the Assembly Diagram, page 43; refer to the diagram and the full-quilt photo, page 42, to plan your fabrics.

- assorted 44-inch-wide cotton or cotton-blend fabrics
- ⅓ yard each 11 blue prints (A and C); 2⅛ yards 60-inch-wide red-and-white 1-inch-wide horizontal striped (B); 1¼ yards 56-inch-wide blue-and-white awning-type stripe (D); ⅛ yard each 18 red prints (E and F)
- 3 yards 90-inch-wide bleached muslin (or sewn-together equivalent) for the back
- full-size quilt batting
- 5 white 10-meter (10.8-yard) skeins DMC matte embroidery cotton or pearl cotton for ties
- darning needle
- rotary cutter and mat (optional)
- straightedge or quilter's ruler
- quilt pins

HOW TO MAKE IT

Note: Before you begin, see *Quilting Basics*, page 176.

1. *Cutting:* For speed and accuracy, cut long strips of fabric the proper width, then cut the strip into shorter lengths as required (¼-inch seam allowance is included in the cutting)

From blue prints (A), fifteen 10½-inch squares

From red stripe (B), two strips each 5½ × 44 inches and 5½ × 64 inches

From blues (C), fifty-four 4½-inch squares

From blue stripe (D), four strips each 4½ × 31 and 4½ × 41 inches with stripes lengthwise; four 4½-inch squares

From reds (E), seventy-eight 4½-inch squares

From reds (F), seventy-eight 4½-inch squares.

2. *Patchwork:* Arrange the fabrics for each section to balance and contrast the prints and color tones before you stitch them together.

Section A: Lay out the 10½-inch blue squares in five rows of three as shown on the Assembly Diagram. Stitch them together in strips of three across. Then stitch the strips together to form the central rectangle of the quilt.

Section B: Attach the B strips to the edges of the rectangle, leaving at least 5½ inches of each

strip extending at each end to miter the corners. Press. To miter the corners: Fold the corner square of the patchwork diagonally toward the outer corner, wrong side out, bringing the border strips together back to back as well. With a pencil and a straightedge, continue the diagonal line from the corner of the patchwork across the strips. Pin and stitch the borders together (wrong side out) along the marked line. Remove the pins and trim the seam allowance to ¼ inch. Press.

Section C: Plan the layout of the C squares around the edge of the borders. Stitch a strip of 10 squares for each end of the patchwork and 17 squares for each side. Stitch a strip to each end of the patchwork, then to the sides.

Section D: Stitch the D squares between pairs of D strips as shown on the Assembly Diagram. Centering the square on each edge, stitch the strips to the patchwork and miter the corners as before.

Sections E and F: Plan the layout of squares in each border. Stitch the squares into strips and attach the E borders, then attach the F borders.

3. *Assembly:* Lay out the back fabric with wrong side facing you. Center the batting then the patchwork right side out on top. Pin (or baste) the layers together smoothly and thoroughly, working from the center out. Trim the back and batting all around to ¾ inch larger than the patchwork.

4. *Binding:* Cut five 2½-inch-wide strips lengthwise from fabric B. Cut one strip in half crosswise. Stitch one half to a long strip with stripes matching, and the other to another long strip to have two strips at least 96 inches long for the sides. Press ¼ inch to the wrong side on one long edge of each strip. With the right sides together, pin and stitch the unpressed edge of the shorter bindings even with the top and bottom edges of the patchwork. Fold the bindings to the back; pin and slipstitch the pressed fold in place. Trim the ends even with the quilt edge if necessary. Bind the sides in the same way, tucking the ends in as you fold the bindings to the back. Sew the ends closed by hand.

5. *Ties:* Remove the basting. Then with pins, mark the corner and center of every square and every 4 inches along the center of the D stripes, through all layers. On the large B squares, also mark the center of each square and the center of each edge. Then mark the corners of an imaginary 5-inch square in the middle of each one. With the darning needle and embroidery cotton,

at each pin take a small stitch through all layers from front to back and to front again. Tie a square knot and trim the ends to ½ inch. Remove the pins.

ASSEMBLY DIAGRAM

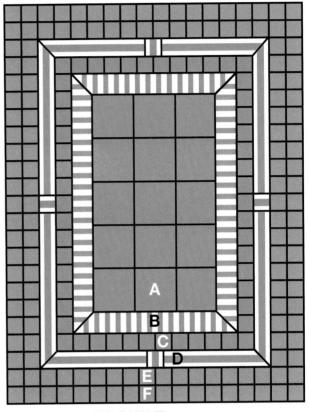

"PATRIOTIC" QUILT

Jiffy Gingham Quilt

❧ ❧ ❧

Six-inch squares in three fabrics form the patchwork. Covered buttons hold the layers together. All you do is stitch straight lines, making this a good first project for beginners and a basic pattern for anyone who wants to stitch a quilt quickly.

SIZES

Throw, 48 × 54 inches; twin, 54 × 72 inches. Changes for twin size are given in brackets [ ]. For a larger quilt, read the directions and add to the number of squares in step 3, opposite. Add 6 inches to the dimensions for each additional row of squares and ¼ yard to the fabric for every 5 additional squares.

Checks and stripes look smart wherever they are, and this variation on the theme makes a vibrant accent on a sofa, chair, or bed.

- medium-weight striped and checked cotton fabrics in variations of one color
- for squares 1 [1¼] yard(s) of 54-inch-wide or 1¼ [1¼] yards of 44-inch-wide each of thin stripe (A), small (⅜-inch) check (B), and large (1⅝-inch) check (C) decorator-weight fabrics
- for back and button covers 2¾ [3] yards 44-inch-wide coordinating miniprint or pin-dot dress-weight fabric
- matching thread
- 24 [36] metal 1-inch-diameter cover buttons (or buttons of your choice)
- quilt batting slightly larger than finished quilt size
- 7-inch cardboard square as a template
- quilt pins

HOW TO MAKE IT

Note: Before you begin, see *Quilting Basics*, page 176.

1. Cut 24 [36] 7-inch squares from fabrics A, B, and C. (To cut easily, first cut 7-inch-wide strips across the width of the fabric, then cut the strips into 7-inch squares using the template.) A ½-inch seam allowance is included in the cutting.

2. Lay out the squares face up in rows of 9 as follows:

Row 1: A B C, A B C, A B C
Row 2: B C A, B C A, B C A
Row 3: C A B, C A B, C A B

Repeat these three rows in sequence until you have 8 [12] rows of 9 squares. Notice that diagonal rows of the same fabrics are formed; this is important for spacing the buttons evenly in the striped squares.

3. With ½-inch seam allowance, stitch the squares together in rows. Then stitch the rows together to form the quilt top. Press the seams open.

4. Fold the backing fabric in half with the raw (44-inch) ends matching. Cut across on the fold. Stitch the two pieces together side by side and press the seam open. With the seam centered across the quilt (not lengthwise), trim the back to the same size as the quilt top.

5. Trim the batting to the same size as the quilt back. Pin or baste the batting securely to the wrong side of the back, placing the pins 2 inches in from the edge. Then trim ⅞ inch off the edges of the batting only.

6. Pin the quilt top to the back with the right sides together. Stitch the quilt top to the backing, with ½-inch seam allowance, leaving one end open. Clip the seam allowance diagonally across the corners. Turn the quilt right side out through the open end. Tuck in and pin the edges of the opening, covering the edge of the batting with one side. Topstitch the opening closed, ½ inch from the edge, and continue around the quilt, catching the edge of the batting in the stitching.

7. Cover the buttons with the remaining backing fabric, *following the button manufacturer's instructions.* Keeping the quilt smooth, place a pin at the center of all A (striped) squares through all thicknesses of the fabric. At each pin, sew a button through all the layers and remove the pins.

Weekend Warmer

❧ ❧ ❧

Make this lively quilt either as a throw for lap or nap or in a larger size as a bedcover. The patches are easily assembled from strips, not tiny squares, and if you can sew a straight seam, you can do it.

SIZES

Throw, 47 × 62 inches; twin, 71 × 86 inches; full/queen, 92 × 92 inches; king, 98 × 98 inches. Changes in instructions for the larger sizes are included in brackets [ ].

YOU WILL NEED

- 44-inch-wide cotton fabrics
- for top, 1¼ [1¾-2-2] yards blue print (B) and 2 [3½-4-4½] yards yellow print (Y)
- for border, 1¾ [2½-2¾-2¾] yards yellow plaid (P)
- for the back, a sheet that fits the final quilt size or 2¾ [4⅛-7⅞-8½] yards of 44-inch-

wide fabric or 1⅞ [4⅛-5¼-5½] yards 54-inch-wide fabric
- quilt batting for quilt size
- 2 large spools of cotton or cotton-wrapped yellow thread
- ¼-inch-wide masking tape
- optional: rotary cutter, mat, and see-through ruler

HOW TO MAKE IT

Note: Before you begin, see *Quilting Basics*, page 176. A ¼-inch seam allowance is included in the cutting.

1. *To make the Nine Patch blocks:* Cut 3-inch-wide × 44-inch-long strips across the fabric width, as follows: 8 [13-15-15] of color B and 7 [11-12-12] of color Y. Cut selvages off the edges.

Stitch the strips together lengthwise in groups of three to make 3 [5-6-6] panels with Y between B, and 2 [3-3-3] panels with B between Y (Diagrams 1A and 1B, below).

Cut across the panels every 3 inches to have strips of three squares (Diagrams 2A and 2B, below)—you need 36 [64-82-82] strips of BYB and 18 [32-41-41] of YBY.

Finally, stitch the short strips together to form 18 [32-41-41] 9-patch blocks about 8 inches square (Diagram 3, below). Trim all blocks to the same size (if any are much too big or small, you can make substitutes from the excess strips).

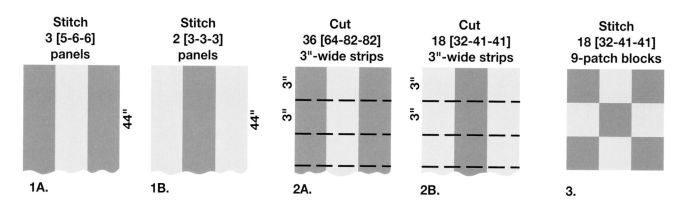

9-PATCH BLOCKS

A traditional Nine Patch design is updated with bright sunny patches and a cool plaid border.

2. *Plain blocks:* Cut 17 [31-40-40] squares of Y the same size as the patched blocks.

3. *Block assembly:* Lay out the patched and plain blocks alternately as on the Assembly Diagram, page 49, for the size you are making. Stitch the blocks together in rows across, then stitch the rows together.

4. *Y Border:* Cut eight 2 [3-4½-5½]-inch-wide strips across 44-inch-wide Y fabric. Piece two strips each together for two sides, top and bottom. Centering the seams, stitch the strips to the long side edges. Trim the ends even with the patchwork. Stitch the borders to the top and bottom, including the ends of the previous borders; trim.

5. *P border:* Cut four 3½ [7-8½-10½]-inch-wide strips from the full length of P. Stitch one strip to each side edge; trim the ends even with the patchwork. Stitch one each to the top and bottom; trim. Press the completed quilt top, taking care not to distort the fabric.

6. *Back:* Cut the backing sheet or fabric about 1 inch larger than the top all around. If it is necessary to piece it, cut the fabric in half crosswise [in thirds for 44-inch-wide fabric for full/queen and king sizes] and stitch the pieces together side by side. Press the seam(s) open. (The seams can be placed crosswise or lengthwise on the quilt, depending on the fit.)

7. *Assembly:* Spread out the back, wrong side up. Center the batting over it smoothly and trim the edges even with the back. Center the patchwork right side up on top. Baste or pin through all the layers, working from the center out in rows 6 inches apart and keeping the fabrics smooth.

8. *Quilting:* Set the machine stitch length for about 12 stitches per inch. Machine-stitch (or hand-stitch) diagonal lines through the blue squares and across the borders (see the sample dashed lines on the Assembly Diagram). Mark guidelines with a disappearing marker, or lay out masking tape for the lines and stitch to the right of the tape. Stitch all the diagonal rows in one direction, then in the opposite direction. End rows at the edges. The binding will cover the ends of the stitching. Finally, trim the batting and back even with the top.

9. *Binding:* Cut 2-inch-wide strips across the B fabric. Stitch the strips end to end to fit around the quilt, plus 8 inches. Fold or press the binding in half lengthwise, right side out. Pin the binding to the quilt top, with the raw edges matching. Stitch ¼ inch from the edge. To turn corners, stop ¼ inch before the corner with needle in the fabric, lift the presser foot, and turn the quilt. Make a small tuck or pleat at the corner and continue stitching. Overlap the ends and turn under the raw end ½ inch (trim the excess) before finishing. Fold the binding to the quilt back; pin and slipstitch the binding in place. To miter the corners, fold the pleat down and finger-press and hand-sew the diagonal edges together. Sew the binding ends closed on the back.

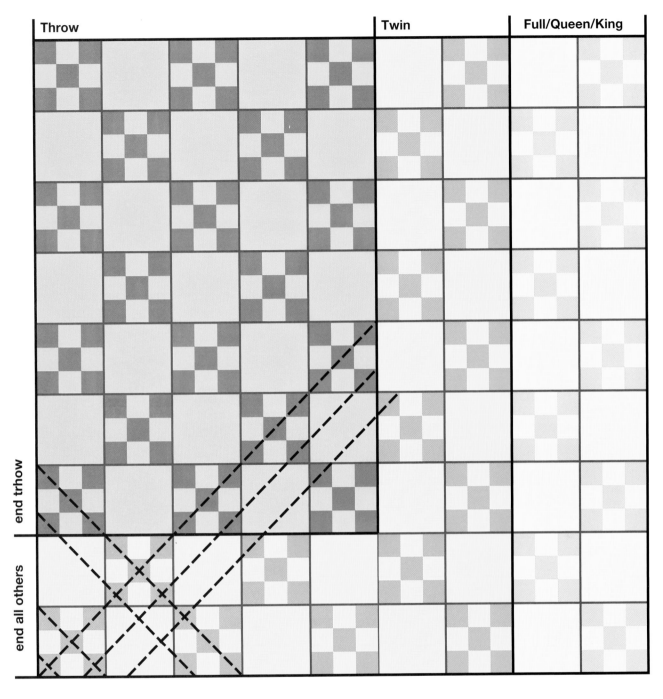

Throw

Twin

Full/Queen/King

end trhow

end all others

— — — — - quilting

WEEKEND WARMER ASSEMBLY DIAGRAM

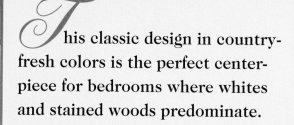

This classic design in country-fresh colors is the perfect centerpiece for bedrooms where whites and stained woods predominate.

Log-Cabin Quilt

❧ ❧ ❧

Six giant blocks made from two versions of the traditional Log Cabin design are fun to assemble for this quilt. We made it in sparkling brights, but if you prefer a darker palette, it adapts.

SIZE

70 × 80 inches for a twin or full-size bed.

YOU WILL NEED

- 44-inch-wide cotton or cotton-blend calico fabrics:
    - 2½ yards each white and blue, 2 yards red, and ½ yard green for the top
    - 4½ yards solid yellow for squares and back
- twin-size quilt batting 81 × 96 inches
- a few yards of white crochet cotton for ties
- embroidery needle
- quilt pins
- ruler and scissors or rotary cutter and pad

HOW TO MAKE IT

Note: Before you begin, see *Quilting Basics*, page 176. The ¼-inch seam allowance is included in the cutting.

1. Cut or tear the yellow fabric in half crosswise into two 2¼-yard lengths. From one half, cut two 15-inch × 2¼-yard lengths. Set the three pieces (one full width and two 15-inch widths) aside for the back.

2. Cut the following calico strips lengthwise for the borders and set them aside.

White: two 7 × 72½ inches and one 7 × 67½ inches

Red: two 4½ × 69½ inches and two 2 × 54½ inches

Blue: two 2 × 79 inches and one 2 × 70½ inches

3. From the remaining fabric, cut:

six 5½-inch yellow squares for block centers

2¾-inch-wide strips lengthwise from all the remaining white-print fabric

six 2¾-inch-wide strips lengthwise from the red fabric

five from the blue, and fourteen from the green.

4. There are six Log Cabin blocks, four with multicolor stripes (X) and two with red-and-white stripes (Y). To make the four X blocks follow the sequence of 16 strips and colors on the upper right-hand block on the Assembly Diagram, page 52. (The X blocks are all made the same and turned in position on the quilt.) To make the Y blocks follow the sequence around the right-hand Y block.

5. Start the blocks by stitching the six yellow squares one after the other to a red strip (see Strip Piecing, Diagram A, below). Cut the red strip apart between units, along the edges of the squares. Press the pieces open on the seams, pressing the seam allowance toward the darker fabric (Diagram B). You have attached strip 1 of a Log Cabin block. Set aside four units for the X blocks.

6. Pin the two Y units to a long red strip of fabric to attach piece 2 (Diagram C). Stitch, cut the strip, and press the unit as before (Diagram D). Continue rotating the sewn units clockwise

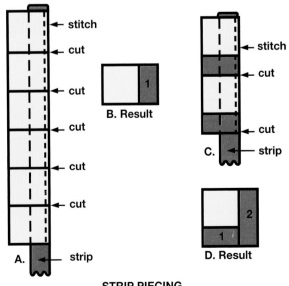

STRIP PIECING

ASSEMBLY DIAGRAM
(All border dimensions are cut sizes.)

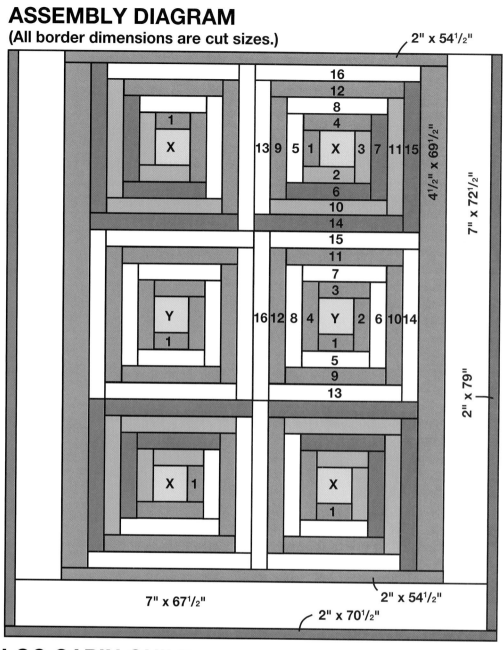

LOG CABIN QUILT

and attaching strips 3 through 16 of the Y blocks, following the Assembly Diagram.

7. Assemble the four multicolor Log Cabin X blocks in the same way.

8. Pin the blocks together side by side in three rows of two, turning the X blocks as on the Assembly Diagram. Make sure the blocks are correctly positioned, then stitch the pairs together. Stitch the rows together.

9. Add the red side borders, then, in this order, the upper and lower red borders, the white side and lower borders, and the blue side and lower borders.

10. Back: Stitch a narrow backing panel to each long edge of the wider backing panel.

11. *Quilt Assembly:* Smooth out the patchwork right side up over the batting and thoroughly baste the pieces together as follows: from the center to the corners, then from the center to the center of each edge, and finally from the center of one edge to the center of the next edge. This forms an X in each quarter.

12. Center and pin the backing to the patchwork with the right sides together. Trim the backing and batting to the same size as the patchwork. Then stitch the edges, leaving a 12-inch opening in one side. Roll the quilt edges toward the opening and push through to turn the quilt right side out. Turn in the raw edges and slipstitch the opening closed.

13. *Ties:* Pin through all the layers at each outer corner of the yellow center squares, at each corner of the concentric Log Cabin squares, then every 4½ inches along the center of the white border. Stitch and tie at each pin as follows: Thread the embroidery needle with doubled crochet thread. Insert the needle from front to back through all the layers, leaving a 3-inch tail on the front. Then take an ⅛-inch-long stitch to the front, stitch to the back next to the tail, and to the front again. Tie a square knot without removing the needle and trim the ends to ¾ inch. Remove all basting.

Autumn Leaves Quilt

❧ ❧ ❧

Fabrics with small prints give life and texture to this quilt. The leaves are ironed on with fusible web to hold them in place while you satin-stitch around the edges. The quilting is quickly done by machine, but you can hand quilt, especially around the leaves, if you prefer.

SIZE

54 × 66 inches for a twin bed, throw, or wall hanging.

YOU WILL NEED

- 44-inch-wide cotton or cotton-blend print fabrics in fall colors:
- ¼ yard each: for leaves red (A), tangerine (B), light gold (C), dark gold (D), orange (E), rust (F), burgundy (G), dark brown (H), and green (I); for checkered corners a slightly different green print (J)
- ¾ yard each red (K) and gold (L) for sashes
- 1½ yards dark green (M) for the binding and green leaf
- 4½ yards white for the blocks and backing
- 72 × 90-inch quilt batting
- thread to match fabrics and large spool of white
- 2 yards paper-backed fusible web
- quilt pins
- water-soluble fabric marker
- rotary cutter, mat, and see-through ruler (optional)
- tracing paper and stiff paper for leaf patterns
- sewing machine with zigzagger

HOW TO MAKE IT

Note: Before you begin, see *Quilting Basics,* page 176.

1. *Cut the fabrics:* From white cut two 30- × 68-inch pieces for backing (set aside) and twenty 10-inch squares for blocks.

From red K and gold L, cut forty-nine 2 × 9½-inch strips of each color for sashes. To cut strips quickly, stack the two fabrics and cut thirteen 2 × 44-inch strips across the width with the rotary cutter. Cut the 9½-inch lengths from the strips.

From white and green J, cut sixty 2-inch squares each for the checked corners.

From dark green M, cut five 3-inch-wide bias strips for the binding. To cut bias strips, fold the top edge of fabric down diagonally, even with one side edge; cut 3-inch-wide strips parallel to the diagonal fold.

2. *Appliqué:* Trace the four leaf patterns, pages 57–58. Cut the fusible web into twenty 7-inch squares and iron the squares onto the back of the assorted fabrics for leaves (see the Assembly photograph, page 56, for suggested colors). Leave the paper backing on the fabrics. Trace five of each leaf in assorted colors, omitting the stems, onto the paper backing. Then cut out the fabric leaves and draw veins on their fronts with the marker. Pin each leaf diagonally to the center of a white block, allowing room for the stems, and iron them in place, *following the web manufacturer's instructions.* With matching thread and ⅛-inch-wide satin stitch on your zigzagger, stitch the stem and center vein. (Backstitch to begin and end each

The leaves are falling—at least it looks as if they are on this marvelous quilt. The simple trick of placing them on the diagonal in each block imparts a sense of motion to the rich fall colors of this design.

row.) With a narrower satin stitch, work the smaller veins and edge of the leaf. Trim the blocks to 9½-inch squares with the leaves centered.

AUTUMN LEAVES QUILT ASSEMBLY

3. *Assembly:* Stitch two 2-inch squares of different colors together for the checkered corners and stitch 2 pairs together to form the corner blocks, alternating colors. With ¼-inch seam allowance (used throughout), stitch the red and gold sashes together in pairs on their long edges.

Then assemble and stitch the top row of checks and sashes as on the Assembly photograph. Stitch together the next row of sashes and blocks. Continue to stitch each crosswise row, then stitch the rows together to form the patchwork top.

4. *Back:* Stitch the white backing pieces together on their long edges. Press the seam allowance open. With the seam crosswise, spread out the back wrong side up. Smooth the quilt batting on top and trim it to match the back. Center the patchwork, face up, over the batting. Baste the layers together, working out from the center to the sides and corners, keeping the fabrics smooth.

5. *Quilting:* Roll the quilt wrong side out lengthwise to fit it under the machine arm. With straight stitches (10 per inch) and white thread, topstitch along the block and sash seams. Then roll the quilt crosswise and stitch the remaining block and sash seams. Finally, baste around the leaves with pins, then stitch around them close to the satin-stitch edging, rolling up and pinning the quilt as needed to work.

6. *Finishing:* Trim the back and batting 1¼ inches larger than the quilt top all around. With the right side of the fabrics together and raw edges of the binding and quilt top matching, pin bias binding to the top and bottom edges of the quilt, slightly stretching the binding as you work. Stitch ¼ inch from the front edges. Trim the ends of the binding even with the back and batting. Fold the binding to the back of the quilt; turn under ¼ inch on the raw edge; pin and slip stitch the binding to the back. Cut one remaining bias strip in half, and stitch one half to the end of each remaining bias strip. Pin the strips to the long edges of the quilt and bind as before, tucking the ends in neatly when you fold the binding to the back. Sew the ends closed by hand.

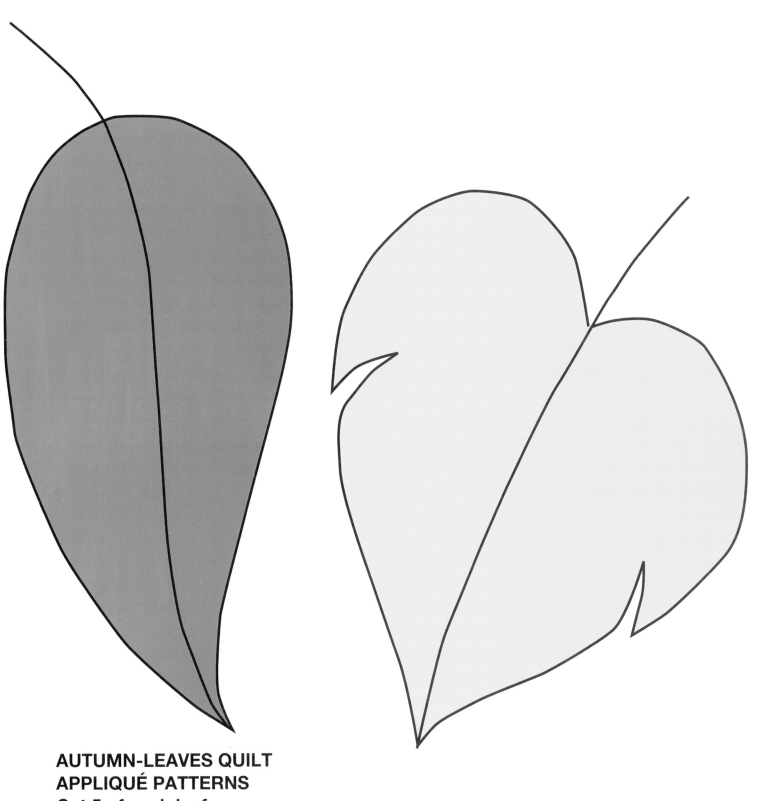

**AUTUMN-LEAVES QUILT
APPLIQUÉ PATTERNS**
Cut 5 of each leaf

**AUTUMN-LEAVES QUILT
APPLIQUÉ PATTERNS**
Cut 5 of each leaf

A plaid quilt seems cozier than any other on a cold winter's night.

Tartan Quilt

❧ ❧ ❧

With its blocks of two stylized, triangular pine trees surrounded by snowy white patches, you know this is a quilt for the three coldest months of the year. You stitch the blocks, plaid squares, and borders together. Add ties and top the trees with festive bows.

SIZE

63 × 81 inches

YOU WILL NEED

◆ 60-inch-wide fabrics: 2 yards red plaid for squares, 2 yards white plaid for borders, and 1 yard green plaid (GP) for trees; 2 yards 44-inch-wide white cotton flannel (WF)

- red twin-size cotton flannel sheet (RF) or equivalent fabric for the back
- 3 yards ¼-inch-wide red satin ribbon
- twin-size quilt batting
- red and white thread
- 2 skeins DMC Pearl Cotton #5, Red 666
- darning needle
- lightweight cardboard for templates
- rotary cutter, mat, and ruler
- quilt pins

Note: Before you begin, see *Quilting Basics*, page 176.

1. From the block pattern, opposite, trace pattern pieces GP, WF, and RF separately on cardboard. Add ¼-inch seam allowance around each one and cut them out to use as templates.

2. Trace the templates onto the backs of fabrics to cut all the pieces for 18 blocks. (*Note:* The three template shapes are repeated on the block more than once and you must cut 18 of each piece shown on the block pattern. If the green plaid for the trees has a distinctive contrasting stripe, plan to have the stripe running down the center of each tree.)

3. Cut out the pieces for the blocks.

4. *Assemble the tree blocks:* Stitch the green and white triangles together in pairs, taking care not to stretch the edges. Then stitch the pairs together to form squares. Stitch the long WF strips to the white edges. Press. Stitch a white strip to each side of the red squares (tree trunks). Then stitch one of these assembled strips to the bottom of each triangular tree. The finished blocks should be squares approximately 9½ inches on each side. Trim them all the same size.

5. Cut 21 red-plaid squares the same size as the trimmed blocks. Try to cut each square from identical sections of the plaid.

6. Starting with a tree block with trunks vertical in the upper left corner, alternate the blocks and squares to lay out a rectangle of five by seven rows. Four plaid squares will be left over for the border. Stitch each row of five pieces, then stitch the rows together.

7. *Borders:* Measure the edges of the assembled squares. For each edge, cut a white-plaid border ½ inch longer than each edge and 9½ inches wide (or the same width as the leftover red-plaid squares). Stitch a red-plaid square to each end of the two short borders (for top and bottom edges). Stitch the side borders, then the top and bottom borders in place.

8. *Assembly:* Cut a red flannel back the same size as the quilt top. Spread out the quilt top smoothly right side up and the backing over it, wrong side up. Place the batting on top and trim it even with the back. Pin the layers firmly together. Stitch around the quilt, ¼ inch from the edges, leaving a 12-inch opening on one side. Clip the seam allowance across the corners. Remove the pins. Turn the quilt right side out, taking care not to pull the batting separately. Turn under ¼-inch edges and slip stitch the opening closed. Finally, topstitch around the entire quilt 1 inch from edges, stopping 1 inch before each corner with the needle in the fabric to turn the corners.

9. *Ties:* Smooth out the quilt and pin through all layers at the corners, the center of the sides, and the center of all the red-plaid blocks. Repeat the same spacing along the centers of the borders. At each pin, with a double strand of pearl cotton in the darning needle, take a stitch from the front through all layers and tie a square knot or double knot on the front. Trim the tie ends to ¾ inch.

10. *Bows:* Cut eighteen 6-inch lengths of ribbon. Tack one by hand or machine in each block between the treetops, sewing through all the layers of the quilt.

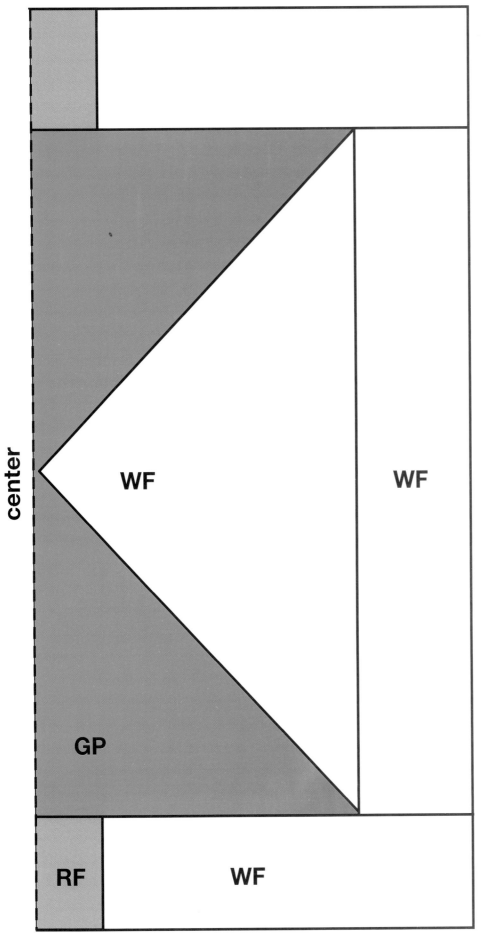

TARTAN QUILT TREE BLOCK

This quilt is ready in a jiffy, easily made with the latest Christmas prints. It's great for bundling up with the family on cold winter nights.

Christmas Quilt

Holiday decorations make festivities merrier. You can make this quilt quickly for the guest room, or for all the family bedrooms. With only four fabric prints and easy squares to stitch, you can whip one up for every season. Inveterate stitchers take note.

SIZE

43 × 56 inches

YOU WILL NEED

- **45-inch-wide cotton or cotton-blend holiday print or other fabrics**
- **5/8 yard each two blue (A and C) and one red (B) calico prints and pin-dot red (D)**
- **1 3/4 yards red fabric for the back**
- **45 × 58-inch piece of quilt batting**
- **9 yards 3/8-inch-wide red satin ribbon**
- **red thread**
- **7-inch cardboard square as a template**
- **rotary cutter, mat, and straightedge**
- **quilt pins**

HOW TO MAKE IT

Note: Before you begin, see *Quilting Basics*, page 176.

1. Cut sixteen 7-inch squares each from prints A, B, and C, and fifteen from D, using the template.

2. Lay out the squares as seen on the Assembly Diagram, right. Then, with right sides of fabrics together, and a 3/8-inch seam allowance, stitch the top two rows of seven squares together to form strips. Stitch the next row together. Press the seam allowances to one side. Then stitch the rows together, matching the seams. Continue making strips and joining them until all are assembled.

3. Lay out the patchwork face up, the backing fabric facedown, and smooth the quilt batting on top. Pin the layers smoothly together. Trim the edges of the back and batting even with the patchwork.

4. Stitch 3/8 inch in from the edge through all layers, leaving a 12-inch opening on one side. Trim the seam allowance and clip it diagonally across the corners. Then turn the quilt right side out through the opening. Gently press the seam to make the edge crisp. Turn in the raw edges and slip stitch the opening closed.

5. Topstitch around the quilt 3/4 inch from the edge.

6. Cut the ribbon into thirty-two 10-inch lengths. Tie bows and trim the ends diagonally. Smooth out the quilt and pin a bow to the center of each blue square. Tack the center of the bows in place through all layers by hand or zigzag-stitch by machine.

A	B	C	D	A	B	C
B	C	D	A	B	C	D
C	D	A	B	C	D	A
D	A	B	C	D	A	B
A	B	C	D	A	B	C
B	C	D	A	B	C	D
C	D	A	B	C	D	A
D	A	B	C	D	A	B
A	B	C	D	A	B	C

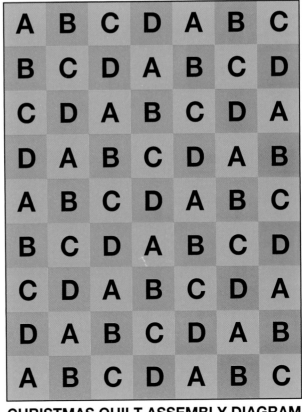

CHRISTMAS QUILT ASSEMBLY DIAGRAM

Quilt Block Afghan

✤ ✤ ✤

The square, colored centers are worked in single crochet stitch from charts for five designs. The squares are then bordered by white, joined together, and finished with clusters of half-double and double crochet stitches.

SIZE

Throw 51 × 60 inches. Changes for a twin or full bedcover 60 × 70 inches are in brackets [ ].

YOU WILL NEED

- Yarn: 3½-oz/100-gram/240-yard skein knitting-worsted-weight: 8 [11] skeins white (A); 1 each gold (B) and dusty rose (C), 1 [2] each rose (D) and teal (E), 1 each grape (F), blue (G), light blue (H), turquoise (I), and yellow (J)
- crochet hook size K (6.50 mm) or the size that gives you the correct gauge
- yarn bobbins (optional)

Gauge: 6 sc = 2 inches; 7 rows sc = 2 inches.
Note: Crochet abbreviations used are listed on page 173.

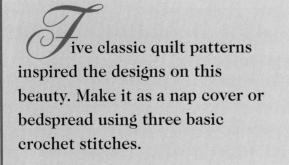

*F*ive classic quilt patterns inspired the designs on this beauty. Make it as a nap cover or bedspread using three basic crochet stitches.

Notes: 1. Work each color section with a separate ball or bobbin of yarn (but when passing only one or two stitches, carry the yarn on top and enclose it in the stitches).

2. Wind a bobbin for each color, or make a butterfly bobbin. (To make a butterfly: Wind yarn around your spread thumb and forefinger; wind and fasten the end around the middle; pull the yarn from the center to work.)

3. *To change color*, work an sc until the last 2 loops remain on the hook, complete the sc with the next color; drop the old color to the wrong side of the work. Leave 3-inch ends to weave in.

HOW TO MAKE IT

Square: Follow the five charts on page 67 to make as many squares of each design as indicated, beginning as follows: Ch 21 in the color of the first row.

Row 1 (right side): Following chart Row 1 for color (each square represents 1 stitch), sc in the top loop of the second ch from the hook and in each ch across (20 sc).

Rows 2 through 20: Ch 1, turn. Sc in each sc across, reading chart rows from right to left (except on chart 5, read the wrong-side rows from left to right). Fasten off after Row 20.

Square Border: Working around each square, crochet all rounds from the right side of the work as follows:

Round 1: Join A in the 12th stitch (st) in the top row; ch 3, double crochet (dc) in same st; *skip the next st, work (half-double crochet [hdc] and dc) in the next st (cluster [cl] made)*; repeat from * to * to the last 2 sts on the top (hdc, dc, and hdc), in the last st (corner made); work a cl in the 3rd row, then in every 2nd row on the side edge (9 cl on side); work (hdc, dc, hdc) in the first ch on the lower edge (corner made); repeat from * to * across the lower edge, ending in the next to last st; (hdc, dc, hdc) in the last st; work 9 cl on the right-side edge as for the left edge; (hdc, dc, hdc) in the first st on the upper edge; work (skip 1 st, cl) 5 times along the edge, ending in the st before ch-3; join with a slip st in the top of ch 3.

Round 2: Ch 3, dc in next dc; sk next st; *cl in the dc of each cl to the next corner, skip the hdc, cl in the center dc at the corner, ch 1 (dc, hdc), in the next hdc at the corner; repeat from * around; join as before.

Round 3: Work same as Round 2, at corners working cl in first dc (dc, ch 1, dc), in ch-1 space, skip the dc (dc, hdc), in the next hdc. To end the round, join as before. Fasten off.

Assembly: Following the diagram opposite, lay out the squares with the right sides facing you, making sure the upper edge of each square is at the top. (For the throw size, omit the right-hand vertical row and bottom row of squares, ending at *'s on the diagram.) Starting at the right-hand edge between the two top rows, join A in the ch at the upper corner of the lower square; ch 2, slip st in the ch at the lower corner of the upper square; *ch 1, slip st in the next st on the lower square, ch 1, slip st in the corresponding st on the upper square; repeat from * across all the squares on the two top rows to join them together. Fasten off. Join all the rows of squares horizontally in the same way. Then work the vertical joinings from bottom to top in the same way, crossing over the previous joinings at the corners.

Afghan Border: Work all rounds from the right side.

Round 1: Attach A at the edge of the afghan in a joining between squares; ch 3, dc in the same place; ** (hdc and dc) in the dc after the corner ch on the next square (cl made); skip 1 st, cl in the hdc of the next cl; *skip 1 st, cl in the dc of the next cl; repeat from * to next joining, cl in joining; repeat from ** to the ch-1 sp at the outer corner of the afghan; in the corner sp work (dc, ch 1, dc, ch 1, and dc), (dc, hdc) in the hdc of the next cl at the corner; continue from *, working as before on all sides. Join with slip st in top of ch 3.

Round 2: Ch 3, dc in the same as the joining, cl in the dc of each cl around, working (hdc and dc) in the first ch 1 sp at corners and (dc, hdc) in the next ch 1 sp. Join; fasten off.

Weave the yarn ends into stitches of matching color on the back.

ASSEMBLY

					*
1	2	3	4	5	1
4	1	5	3	2	4
3	5	4	2	1	3
2	3	1	5	4	2
5	4	2	1	3	5
1	2	3	4	5	1
*					
4	1	5	3	2	4

QUILT BLOCK AFGHAN

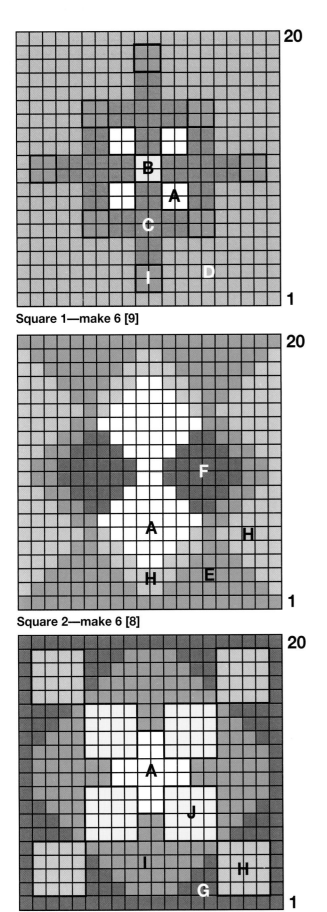

Square 1—make 6 [9]

Square 2—make 6 [8]

Square 3—make 6 [8]

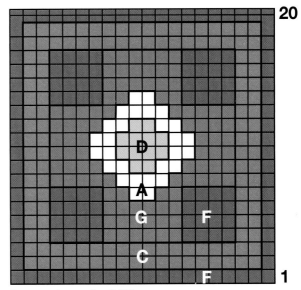

Square 4—make 6 [9]

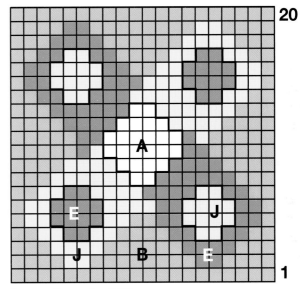

Square 5—make 6 [8]

QUILT BLOCK AFGHAN

Plaid Afghan

❦ ❦ ❦

This afghan is worked in one piece in double crochet stitches in three colors. Use blues and red, as we did, or select a light and dark shade of any color for the squares and an accent color for the stripes.

SIZE

38 × 60 inches

YOU WILL NEED

◆ **Coats & Clark's Red Heart Classic (3½-ounce, 100-gram skein acrylic 4-ply worsted-weight yarn) or similar yarn: 5 skeins each Country Red 914 (R), Windsor Blue 808 (B), and Pale Pale Blue 815 (C)**
◆ **crochet hook size G (4.50 mm) or the size that gives you the correct gauge**
◆ **14 large yarn bobbins**

Gauge: 11 dc = 3 inches
Note: Crochet abbreviations used are listed on page 173.

Notes: 1. Chain 3 to turn after each row. The turning chain counts as the first dc. **2.** Do not carry yarn across the blocks; use a separate ball or bobbin for each color and carry the balls or bobbins on the wrong side of the work. **3.** *To change color;* work a dc until the last 2 loops remain on the hook, complete the dc with the next color; drop the old color to the wrong side.

HOW TO MAKE IT

Afghan: With color R, ch 135.
Row 1 (right side): Dc in the fourth ch from the hook and in each ch across (132 dc, counting ch 3 at beginning).

Row 2: Ch 3, turn (first dc made); dc in next dc, changing to color C; *with C work (2 dc C, 2 dc B) twice, then work 2R, 2C, 2R, (2B, 2C) 5 times, 2R, 2B, 2R; repeat from * twice more; work (2C, 2B) twice, 2R.

Rows 3, 4, and 5: Repeat Row 2 to work R over R, B over C, and C over B on each row.

Row 6: Dc across with R.

Row 7: Work 2 dc R, *(2B, 2C) twice, 2R, 2C, 2R, 20C, 2R, 2C, 2R (2B, 2C), twice, 2R*; 2B, 2R, 20B, 2R, 2B, 2R; repeat from * to * once more.

Row 8: Dc with R.

Rows 9 through 20: 2R, *(2C, 2B) twice, 2R, 2C, 2R, 20B, 2R, 2C, 2R, (2C, 2B) twice, 2R*, 2B, 2R, 20C, 2R, 2B, 2R; repeat from * to * once more.

Row 21: Dc with R.

Row 22: Repeat Row 7.

Row 23: Dc with R.

Rows 24 through 28: Repeat Rows 2 through 6.

Row 29: 2R, *(2B, 2C) twice, 2R, 2B, 2R, 20B, 2R, 2B, 2R, (2B, 2C) twice, 2R*, 2C, 2R, 20C, 2R, 2C, 2R; repeat from * to * once.

Row 30: Dc with R.

Rows 31 through 42: 2R, *(2C, 2B) twice, 2R, 2B, 2R, 20C, 2R, 2B, 2R, (2C, 2B) twice, 2R,* 2C, 2R, 20B, 2R, 2C, 2R; repeat from * to * once.

Row 43: Dc with R.

Row 44: Repeat Row 29.

Row 45: Dc with R. Repeat Rows 2 through 45 once more, then Rows 2 through 28 once more.

Edging: Round 1 (right side): Ch 1, turn. With R, sc in each dc across upper edge, work 1 sc in the corner, work 5 sc over every 3 dc along the side, 1 sc in corner; continue across the bottom and other side; slip st in the first sc; do not turn.

Round 2 (right side): Sc in each sc from left to right around for reverse sc, working 3 sc in each corner; slip st in first st. Fasten off. Weave in the ends on the back.

"Afghan" doesn't always mean a cozy throw in delicate pastels. This handsome, peppy plaid would even be welcome in a boy's room.

Mosaic Afghan

❧ ❧ ❧

There is only one block pattern for this afghan, but it's repeated in five color combinations to make a dazzling full-size cover for a twin bed or a throw for a larger bed or sofa. Worked in single crochet throughout, it's easy to make and very warm as well.

SIZE

62 × 74 inches

YOU WILL NEED

- yarn: knitting-worsted-weight (3½-ounce, 100-gram skeins): 7 skeins black (MC), 3 skeins each royal blue (color A), medium green (B), turquoise (C), and violet (D); 2 each gold (E), maroon (F), magenta (G), and fuchsia (H)
- crochet hook size H (5.00 mm) or the size that gives you the correct gauge
- tapestry needle for yarn

Gauge: Each block is 10 inches square.

Note: Crochet abbreviations used are listed on page 173.

HOW TO MAKE IT

Note: For best results, we recommend a wool yarn for easy blocking. On two-color rows, work each color section with separate balls of yarn. *To change color,* work an sc until the last 2 loops remain to be worked, complete the sc with the next color; drop the old color to the wrong side of the work. *To decrease 1 sc,* draw up a loop in each of the next 2 sc, yo and through all 3 loops on the hook.

Blocks: Following the directions for the Basic Block, below, and the diagram, page 73, for place-

ment of colors, make six blocks each in the following colors:

Block 1: Work sections w with D, x with H, y with E, and z with B.

Block 2: Work section w with F, x with E, y with C, and z with G.

Block 3: Work section w with A, x with H, y with D, and z with C.

Block 4: Work section w with B, x with F, y with C, and z with D.

Block 5: Work section w with E, x with G, y with H, and z with A.

Center (section w on block diagram): With the w color, ch 4. Join with a slip st to form a ring.

Round 1 (right side): Ch 1, work (3 sc in ring, ch 1) 4 times; join with a slip st in top of the first sc. *Work all rounds from the right side; do not turn.*

Round 2: Ch 1, * sc in 3 sc (sc, ch 1, sc), in corner ch 1 sp; repeat from * 3 times more; join as before.

Rounds 3 through 9: Ch 1; starting in the same sc as the joining, * sc in each sc to next corner space (sc, ch 1, sc), in corner space; repeat from * 3 times more, sc to the end of the round (you have 19 sc on each side at the end of Round 9); join. Fasten off.

2-color triangles (sections x and y): With right side of work facing you, attach the color for the x section to the first sc on one side of the center square.

Row 1: With x, sc in each of the first 9 sc; with y, sc in the next sc; with another ball of x, sc in the last 9 sc along the same side.

Row 2: Ch 1, turn. With x, dec 1 sc over the first 2 sts, sc in next 6 sc; with y work 3 sc; with x, sc in next 6 sc, dec 1 sc over last 2 sts.

Row 3: Ch 1, turn. With x, dec 1 sc, then work 4 sc; with y, work 5 sc; with x work 4 sc, dec 1 sc.

Row 4: Ch 1, turn. With x, dec 1 sc, work 2 sc; with y work 7 sc; with x work 2 sc, dec 1 sc.

Row 5: Ch 1, turn. With x, dec 1 sc; with y, work 9 sc; with x, dec 1 sc. Fasten off x. Now work with y only.

Row 6: Ch 1, turn. Dec 1 sc, work 7 sc, dec 1 sc.

Rows 7 through 9: Ch 1, turn. Dec 1 sc at each end of every row until 3 sc remain.

Row 10: Ch 1, turn. Draw up a loop in each of next 3 sc, yo and draw through all loops on the hook. Fasten off. Repeat sections x and y on each side of the center square to form a 7-inch square.

Corners (z sections): With the right side of the work facing you, attach z color to a corner of the square.

Row 1: Working into the ends of the rows, work 25 sc evenly spaced across one side of the square.

Row 2: Ch 1, turn. Dec 1 sc, sc to the last 2 sc, dec 1 sc. Repeat Row 2 until 3 sc remain.

Last row: Draw up a loop in each of the 3 sc, yo and draw through all loops on the hook. Fasten off.

Short Joining Strip (make 25): With MC, ch 6. Row 1: Sc in the second ch from the hook and in each remaining ch (5 sc). Row 2: Ch 1, turn. Sc in each sc across. Repeat Row 2 until the strip is 10 inches long (about 40 rows). Fasten off.

Block Assembly: Pin the pieces to matching sizes on a padded surface. Lightly steam wool under a damp cloth and let it dry, or let synthetic yarns dry under the cloth (do not steam synthetics as they tend to go limp). Following the Assembly Diagram, page 73, lay out the blocks as numbered in vertical rows with the short joining strips between them. With the tapestry needle and MC, sew the pieces together to form five lengthwise rows of six blocks, matching the centers and corners of the units carefully. For the neatest joining, sew the edges together on the wrong side, sliding the needle under the back loops of the stitches to butt the edges.

Long Joining Strips (make 4): Note: For the small

BLOCK DIAGRAM

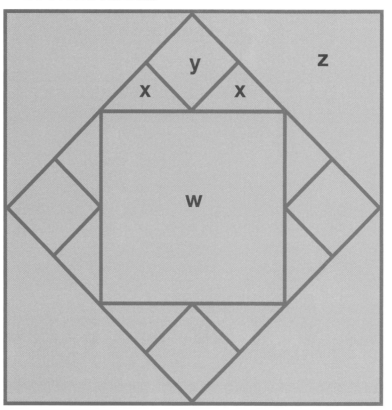

MOSAIC AFGHAN

colored squares on these strips, follow the colors on the Assembly Diagram, or use any color not used on the corners of the adjacent blocks. Work 10 inches (or 40 rows) MC as for the short borders, * then work 6 rows of the desired color for the square, 10 inches of MC (or 40 rows); repeat from * 4 times more. Fasten off.

Sew the long strips between the five rows of blocks to form the afghan.

Top and Bottom Borders (make 2): Work the diamonds (CC) in whatever colors you like. Plan ahead to avoid using colors in the adjacent block and scatter the colors as evenly as possible.

With MC, ch 12.

Row 1: Sc in the second ch from the hook and in each remaining ch (11 sc).

Row 2: Ch 1, turn. Sc in each sc across. Repeating Row 2 for the stitch pattern, work the diamond pattern as follows:

Row 3: Sc across with MC.

Row 4: 5 MC, 1 CC, 5 MC.
Row 5: 4 MC, 3 CC, 4 MC.
Row 6: 3 MC, 5 CC, 3 MC.
Row 7: 2 MC, 7 CC, 2 MC.
Row 8: 1 MC, 9 CC, 1 MC.
Row 9: Repeat Row 7.
Row 10: Repeat Row 6.
Row 11: Repeat Row 5.
Row 12: Repeat Row 4.
Rows 13, 14, and 15: Repeat Row 3.

Repeat Rows 3 through 15 until 16 diamonds are completed, then work three rows MC. Fasten off. Block the borders and sew them to the top and bottom of the afghan.

Side Borders: Work as for the top and bottom borders, but work only one row MC at each end and 21 diamonds with 4 MC. Block, then sew the borders to the sides of the afghan, including the ends of the top and bottom borders.

ASSEMBLY DIAGRAM

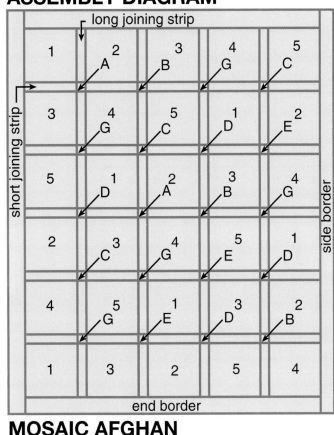

MOSAIC AFGHAN

Christmas Rose Afghan

❧ ❧ ❧

The basic squares for the throw are easy to make in double crochet stitches and are joined together as you go. The leaves are worked in the spaces; the roses are made separately and sewn to the leaves.

SIZE

32 × 45 inches. The afghan can be made larger with an extra ball of white for every six additional squares, and one more of red and green for any size.

YOU WILL NEED

◆ Coats & Clark's Red Heart Classic (3½-oz/99-gram skein 4-ply worsted-weight Orlon acrylic) or similar yarn: 5 skeins Off White (MC), 3 each Country Red (R) and Forest Green (G)
◆ crochet hook size F (4.00 mm) or the size that gives you the correct gauge
◆ large tapestry needle for yarn

Gauge: Two 3 dc groups = 1½ inches; each square is about 6 inches across.

Note: Crochet abbreviations used are listed on page 173.

HOW TO MAKE IT

First Granny Square: Starting at the center, with MC ch 5, slip st in the first ch to form a ring.

Round 1 (right side): Ch 3 (first dc made); in the ring work 2 dc, then (ch 3 and 3 dc) 3 times, ch 3; join with a slip st in the top of the ch 3 (12 dc).

Round 2: Turn. In the first ch 3 sp work a slip st and ch 3 (for the first dc), 2 dc, ch 3 and 3 dc; ch 1, *in the next ch 3 sp work (3 dc, ch 3, 3 dc), ch 1; repeat from * around; join as before. *(Note: From now on, work a slip st and ch 3 in the first space to make the first dc on every round.)*

Round 3: Turn. Work, 3 dc in the first ch 1 sp, ch 1, *(3 dc, ch 3, 3 dc) in the next ch 3 sp (corner made), ch 1, 3 dc in the next ch 1 sp, ch 1; repeat from * around; join.

Round 4: Turn. Work *(3 dc, ch 1) in each ch 1 sp to the corner (3 dc, ch 3, 3 dc), in the ch 3 corner sp, ch 1; repeat from * around; join.

Round 5: Repeat Round 4. Fasten off MC.

Round 6 (right side): With the right side of the work facing you, join G in the first ch 1 sp after a corner, work *(3 dc, ch 1) in each ch 1 sp to the next corner (four 3-dc groups made), ch 3, 3 sc in the corner sp, ch 3; repeat from * around; join in the first dc. Fasten off.

Second Square: Work as for the first square until you've completed the 3 sc in the first corner of Round 6; with wrong sides together, hold the previous square in back; ch 2, sc in the second ch 3 corner sp on the back square; *3 dc in the next ch 1 sp on the front square, sc in the next ch 1 sp on the back square; repeat from * twice more, 3 dc in next ch 1 sp on the front square, sc in next ch 3 sp on the back square, ch 2; 3 sc in ch 3 sp on the front square; ch 3, complete Round 6 of the first granny square from * on the front square.

Remaining squares: Make and join squares to have 7 rows of 5 squares (35 squares). When joining two sides of the squares on the second

The little rose-covered throw could be the centerpiece of your holiday decorations and is sure to be very welcome when the fire burns low.

through seventh rows, end the first joined side ch 2 (instead of ch 3) and join the second side as before. Then complete the front square.

Leaf (make 48): Crochet leaves at the corners where four squares meet as follows:

Row 1: With the right side of the afghan facing you and a row of 5 squares at the bottom, join G in the first of 3 sc in the upper right-hand corner of the second square on the first row (see the diagram, below); ch 3, dc in the same sc, dc in the next sc on the square, 2 dc in the third sc (5 sc).

Row 2: Ch 3, turn. Dc in first dc on the leaf, dc in next 3 dc, 2 dc in last st (7 dc).

Row 3: Turn. Slip st in the second st, ch 3, dc in the next 4 sts (5 dc).

Row 4: Turn. Slip st in the second st, ch 3; holding the last loop of each dc on the hook, dc in the next 2 dc, yo and through all 3 lps on the hook. Fasten off leaving a 10-inch end. Pass the end around the corner ch on Round 2 of the same square and secure it on the back of the leaf with a slip st. Fasten off. On the same corner, working in the first square on Row 2, make a leaf to have a pair of diagonally placed leaves. In the same way, work leaves at the three remaining joined corners between the first 2 rows of squares. Work leaves in the opposite direction on the corners of squares between afghan rows 2 and 3. Continue throughout the afghan, reversing the direction of the leaves on each row.

Rose (make 24): Starting at the center with R, ch 5; slip st in the first ch to form a ring.

Round 1 (right side): Ch 1, work 12 sc in the ring; join with a slip st in top of the first sc. Work all rounds from the right side.

Round 2: (Ch 3, skip 1 sc, sc in next sc) 6 times, join (6 loops made).

Round 3: Slip st in the first ch 3 loop, *ch 1, work 3 dc, ch 1 and slip st in the same loop; slip st in next loop; repeat from * around; join (6 petals made).

Round 4: *Ch 4, slip st in the horizontal thread at the back of the sc on Round 2 between the next 2 petals; repeat from * around, end ch 4, join (6 loops made).

Round 5: Slip st in the first ch 4 loop, *ch 2, work (6 tr, ch 2, slip st) in the same loop, slip st in the next loop; repeat from * around; join. Fasten off leaving a 20-inch end. Center the roses over the leaves and sew their undersides to the corners of the squares.

Edging: Round 1: From the right side of the afghan, join R in the first ch 1 sp at the upper right-hand corner; ch 3, work 2 dc in the same sp, *ch 1, work (3 dc and ch 1) in each ch 1 sp to the next corner of the square, 3 dc in the ch 3 sp, ch 3, sc in each of 3 sc, ch 1, sc in each of 3 sc on the next square, ch 3, 3 dc in the next ch 3 sp; repeat from * around, working (ch 3, sc in 3 sc, ch 3) at the outer afghan corners; join.

Round 2: Ch 1, do not turn; sc from *left to right* for reverse sc in each dc, working 3 sc in the ch 3 sps. Fasten off.

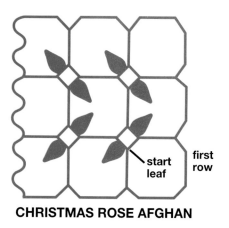

CHRISTMAS ROSE AFGHAN

PAINTED CHAIRS

Folk Art Chair

✧ ✧ ✧

This charming chair will be at home wherever you put it. The paint is easy-to-use acrylic, the seat stitching all straight lines, the hand painting simple. Copy this chair or design one based on your own house. You can omit the sewing and just paint the chair, or make only the seat (the pattern is also good for a separate cushion).

YOU WILL NEED

- a wooden chair with a removable seat that can be covered, or ¼-inch-thick plywood for a new seat
- fabric scraps for the patchwork house (see pattern, page 81)
- quilt batting or 1-inch-thick foam rubber for padding
- acrylic paint for the chair (FolkArt Periwinkle)
- acrylic paints for the decorated rail (FolkArt Calico Red, Camel, Clover and Green Meadow, School Bus Yellow, Sky Blue, Burnt Sienna, Licorice, and Wicker White by Plaid Enterprises)

A bright coat of paint is livelier and easier to do than stripping and restoring the finish on an old chair. And why not make it extra special with a patchwork seat and scenic painted detail.

- sandpaper
- white primer
- 1-inch flat brush for painting chair
- ⅜-inch flat and No. 2 round brushes for design
- fine, black permanent felt-tip marker
- transfer paper
- small sponge
- staple gun or glue gun
- wood screws to attach seat
- clear paste wax

HOW TO MAKE IT

Note: Before you begin painting, see *Furniture Preparation*, page 174.

1. Cut plywood to cover the seat, or remove the old seat and covering.

2. Apply one coat of primer to the chair, then two coats of acrylic paint, letting each coat dry.

3. To stitch the patchwork seat cover: Enlarge the pattern (see *How to Enlarge Patterns*, page 174), extending the edge pieces to the width or length indicated. Trace each piece on the back of the appropriate-color fabric. Add ¼-inch seam allowance around the edges. Then cut the fabric pieces. With the right sides of the fabric together, stitch the A, B, and C sections in sequence. Then stitch the assembled A, B, and C sections together. Add pieces D, E, F, G, H, and I. Press the seam allowances toward the edges.

4. To paint the scene on the chair back: Trace the house directly from the patchwork pattern or enlarge it to the desired size on a photocopier (omit the seam lines on the blue side). Transfer the house to the chair back with transfer paper. Sketch the tree trunks with pencil. Testing the colors first on paper, with the ⅜-inch brush make strokes of blue and white for the sky and Clover Green for the hills and grass. Let the paint dry. With the fine brush, paint the tree trunks Molasses. Paint the house, following the patchwork pattern and the photograph for colors. With the sponge, dab on green leaves and bushes in Green Meadow. When these are dry, highlight them with Clover, the lighter green, and a green mixed with yellow. With the marker, draw a door-knob and outline the window and panes.

5. Paint the chair spindles a green to match the scene. Let the paint dry.

6. With a soft, clean cloth, rub wax over the entire chair. Buff with another cloth before the wax is dry.

7. Cover the plywood seat with thick batting 1 inch larger or foam rubber to fit. Smooth the patchwork on top and staple or glue the edges to the underside, securing the center of each side first and pulling the fabric taut. Fold the corners neatly and complete the stapling.

8. Install the seat with screws from below or as required for your chair.

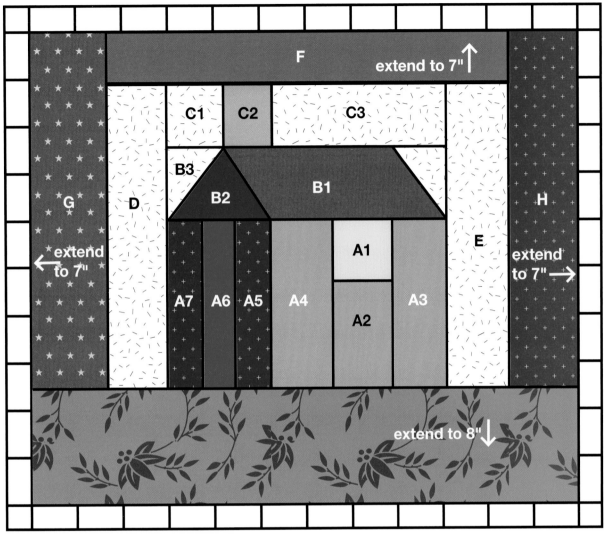

FOLKART CHAIR SEAT

Each square = 1"

Julia Morrill, who designed this chair, loves to turn "sad chairs" into intricate works of art. She christened this one the "world chair" because her friends and neighbors thought it looked African, Spanish, Mexican, Cajun, Indian, and more, "which proves," she says, "that art is universal."

"World" Chair

∓∓ ∓∓ ∓∓

This complex-looking design is simply made with patches of color, then each patch is decorated with dots and lines. Both techniques allow for spontaneity within a basic orderly system.

YOU WILL NEED

- ◆ an old wooden or metal chair
- ◆ interior/exterior latex enamel paints in red, yellow, blue, green, black, and white
- ◆ white acrylic (or metal) primer
- ◆ small flat and round paintbrushes (hobby sets are available in craft and hardware stores)
- ◆ sandpaper
- ◆ tack cloth
- ◆ tape measure

HOW TO MAKE IT

Note: Before you begin, see *Furniture Preparation*, page 174.

1. Brush primer on the chair and let it dry.

2. For the symmetrical design shown, mark the vertical center line on the seat and lightly outline in pencil rows of 3-inch-square patches out to the sides. Stretch or narrow the shapes as you get near the edges. Again, starting at the centers, make 3-inch-long stripes on the back, legs, and rails.

3. Lightly write a color name in each patch to make sure two squares of the same color won't be next to each other.

4. Paint the patches with a flat brush. You can leave a very narrow space between colors; these will be covered later by a black line. And don't worry about precise straight edges; you want a handmade look. Let the paint dry. Paint a second coat if necessary.

5. With a thin brush, paint a black line about ¼ inch wide between the colors overlapping their edges. Decorate the patches with wavy, diagonal, zigzag, grid, or other black lines. Let the lines dry.

6. Paint white dots along the black lines with the tip of a round brush or the brush handle or with an unused pencil eraser.

*T*wo coats of fabric dye give this garden bench its delicate charm.

Dye-Stained Bench

❦ ❦ ❦

Inexpensive, quick and easy to use, dyes invite experimentation and yield surprises. And if you don't like the result, you can just paint over them.

YOU WILL NEED

- an unfinished bench
- 1 or 2 bottles of Rit Liquid Dye for each color
- 1 bottle Rit Liquid Dye in Ecru for antiquing effects
- notebook
- fine and medium-grade sandpapers
- cheesecloth
- flat and round paintbrushes
- cellulose household sponges
- paste furniture wax (or clear polyurethane or exterior finish for outdoor furniture)
- glass or porcelain bowls

HOW TO MAKE IT

Note: Before you begin, see *Furniture Preparation*, page 174.

1. Plan simple figurative or abstract designs of full-strength colors brushed over light ones. It's important to have a plan because changes you make as you go can't be erased and must be worked into the design.

2. Test the dyes and designs on the back of the furniture or on scrap wood of the same kind and grain. Even with this precaution, results on different pieces of wood will differ slightly, so be prepared to intensify or weaken the color.

3. *To test the color:* Mix two parts water (2 capfuls from the dye bottle cap) and one part dye (1 capful) in the glass or porcelain container. Jot down and number the colors and proportions in a notebook. With a brush, saturate a section of the scrap wood with your mixture and number it. Wait for the dye to dry to see the true color. To change the proportions, add more dye for richer color and more water for a paler color. Experiment: Try two coats of the same color, one color over another, or premixed colors. Practice drawing over dry or wet color. Notice whether the lines spread or go on fairly clean.

TESTING COLOR

4. Mix about 2 cups of the final dye selection for a large piece of furniture. Brush the background color onto the wood. To soften the color, you can wipe off some dye with a damp sponge.

5. When the background is dry, add surface designs with full-strength dye on a brush.

6. For an antique finish, lightly rub the piece with medium sandpaper to reveal some of the wood. Brush on a coat of diluted Ecru dye and let it dry.

7. When the color is completely dry (wait at least 72 hours), seal the surface with furniture wax or polyurethane.

DYE STAINING

Stenciled Chair
with Bandanna Quilt

❧ ❧ ❧

Although blue and white look fresh anywhere, if they won't work for you, why not stencil a dark set of chairs for the dining or living room, or a floral one for the bedroom. You can use our pattern or a purchased stencil. The quilt is easy to make in a jiffy, and the simple design is adaptable to calico, flannel, or jersey squares as well as bandannas.

Chair

YOU WILL NEED

- an old or unfinished wooden chair
- primer
- white latex eggshell finish or flat paint
- medium blue acrylic paint (FolkArt True Blue by Plaid Enterprises)
- waxed stencil paper or stencil acetate half-length or full-size of the top chair rail
- craft knife (X-Acto)
- ½-inch stencil brush
- flat paintbrush for chair
- small round synthetic bristle brush for accents
- masking tape
- medium and fine sandpaper
- plastic plate (for the paint)

HOW TO MAKE IT

Note: Before you begin, see *Furniture Preparation*, page 174. Then cover any areas you want to protect, such as the seat, with taped-on newspaper or plastic.

1. Brush primer on the wood and let it dry. Sand the wood lightly.

2. Apply two or three coats of white paint, letting each coat dry and sanding lightly between the coats.

3. See *Stenciling Basics*, page 177. With a pencil, outline the half pattern on the stencil material, or cut a stencil for the whole pattern, if you prefer, by turning the stencil over and aligning it at the center to trace the other half. Remove the stencil. Trace the dot pattern separately.

4. Cut out the stencil designs with the craft knife.

5. Lightly sand the area you're going to stencil and lay the chair on its back to work. Mark the center of the slat lightly. Tape the stencil in place, aligned with the center. You need only a little paint on the stencil brush. Stipple the paint through the stencil onto the chair, working from the edges in, and leaving the centers lighter. Carefully lift off the stencil. If you are using a half stencil, wipe any wet paint off the edges so you can turn it over to paint the other half.

6. When the paint is dry, stencil the other half of the design.

7. Divide the width of the middle slat into quarters. Lightly rule in ¼-inch-wide zigzag lines as shown in the photograph opposite, and mask the edges with tape. Center and mask horizontal lines on the lowest slat. Press the tape down firmly. Mark for stenciled dots with a pencil, then paint the lines and dots with the stencil brush.

8. Accent the wood turnings with stripes and dots as shown.

Bandanna Quilt

SIZE

60 × 60 inches.

YOU WILL NEED

- 21-inch square or larger bandannas: 3 each of red, tan, and blue
- 3½ yards of 44-inch-wide muslin or other fabric for the back
- 62-inch square of quilt batting or 3½ yards of 45-inch-wide batting

You're stuck in the house and cabin fever is on the rise. Could there be a better time for two bright craft projects? Give a flea-market find a bright new personality with a coat of white paint and stencil patterns that mimic Delft pottery. Then stitch up an easy, complementary quilt from bandannas.

- thirteen ⅞-inch flat black buttons
- white thread
- tracing paper (with grid lines if possible)
- 1⅜-inch roundhead straight pins

1. Cut a 21-inch square from the tracing paper as a pattern to even out the bandannas. Place the pattern over each bandanna, centering the design. Trim the edges of the bandanna to make a true 21-inch square if necessary.

2. Lay out the bandannas in three rows of three, rotating the colors (for example: a top row of red, tan, blue; a second row of tan, blue, red; and a third row of blue, red, tan). With the right sides of the fabrics together and a ½-inch seam allowance, stitch the bandannas together to make three strips. Press the seams open. Then stitch the strips together to complete the top. Press the seams open.

3. Fold the backing fabric in half with the raw (44-inch) ends matching. Cut across on the fold. Then stitch the two pieces together, side by side.

Press the seam open. Trim the back to form a 62-inch square (or a size slightly larger than your quilt top).

4. Cut or piece together a 62-inch square of batting, or the size for your quilt. Trim any seam allowance close to the stitching.

5. Pin the batting smoothly to the wrong side of the assembled bandannas and baste the layers together 2 inches from the edges.

6. Pin the backing to the bandannas with the right sides together. Place pins 1 inch apart along the edge and as needed in the middle to keep the fabrics from slipping. Trim the edges of the batting and back to match the bandannas.

7. Stitch through all the thicknesses ½ inch from the edge, leaving a 20-inch opening. Remove the pins. Turn the quilt right side out by rolling it through the opening. Turn in the raw edges of the opening and press all the edges. Sew the opening closed by hand.

8. Pin the layers together in the center of each bandanna and where their corners meet. Sew a button at each pin through all thicknesses and remove the pins.

center

DOT PATTERN

CHAIR-BACK PATTERN

STENCILED CHAIR

PILLOWS

——⚜——

The shortest distance between dull and dashing is a straight line.

Stripe It Rich

✣ ✣ ✣

These simple pillows dressed in bags and bands of stripes look best in a plain room, where they star as peppy accents. Work from a basic group of colors (lay out swatches in the room to decide on the best choices before you buy fabrics or pillows). For maximum zest, choose two closely related colors, such as green and blue or red and orange, and add bright contrasts such as gold and magenta.

YOU WILL NEED

- solid-color or striped pillows or, to make pillows, a pillow form, fabric for each side of the form plus ½-inch seam allowance all around, optional ¼-inch-thick welting cord for the perimeter, and a 1½-inch-wide fabric strip to cover the cord
- ½ yard striped or solid color fabric for bags or bands
- two 1-inch-wide grosgrain ribbons to fit around the pillow, plus 12 inches each for ties, or ribbons of the desired width (as for layered ribbons on the bag at the far right)
- thread
- fabric glue or fusible tape

HOW TO MAKE IT

1. *To make the basic pillow* cut two pieces of fabric ½ inch larger than the pillow form all around. Cut 1½-inch-wide strips of fabric to cover the welting cord; fold the fabric right side out over the cord; stitch close to the cord. Pin the cord to the right side of the cover front with raw edges matching. Lap the ends and turn outward. Baste about ⅛ inch from the welt. Pin the cover back piece to the front piece, with right sides together, and the cord in between. Stitch along the sides between the basting and the welt, leaving an opening for stuffing. Turn the cover right side out. Insert the pillow form. Turn in the raw edges and sew the opening closed.

2. *Striped bag cover.* Make a bag as for the pillow cover, above, omitting the welting and leaving one side open. (The bag can also be made from one piece of fabric folded in half and seamed along the sides.) Turn under the open edge so that about ¼ of the pillow will show when in the bag. Glue or fuse the turned-under fabric in place.

3. *Bands.* If you're not making a bag, tie two 1-inch-wide ribbons parallel around the bag, tie the ends at the top and trim them diagonally (as shown at the center). Or layer two ribbons to make bands (far left) and tack the ends together at the back. Or cut a band of fabric (more than half the pillow width) to slip around the pillow (right). Stitch the ends together to form a circle. Glue or fuse ½-inch hems at the sides of the circle. Slip the band over the pillow and wrap ribbon around the center.

Apple and Pear Pillows
and Fleece Throw

The shaped pear and apple pillows are easy to make in fleece, felt, flannel, or wool, and cotton scraps. They'd be adorable in calico. The painted pillow is stamped with purchased cutout sponges, but you could easily cut your own instead. For the throw, you can buy one ready-made, or cut one from fleece fabric, then give it a border of appliquéd pears and apples.

Apple and Pear-Shaped Pillows

HOW TO MAKE THEM

1. Enlarge the patterns for the apple, pear, and leaf, page 94 (see *How to Enlarge Patterns*, page 174).

2. Place the fruit pattern on fabric folded wrong side out to cut the back and front at the same time. Cut one leaf from checked fabric for each pillow with pinking shears.

3. With the right side of the fabrics together, stitch the edges with ¼-inch seam allowance, leaving the bottom open. Clip the seam allowance on the curves and turn the pillow right side out. Stuff with fiberfill and sew the opening closed.

4. Cut a 2 × 7-inch piece for each stem from brown fabric. Fold them in half, wrong side out, with the 2-inch ends together. Stitch the sides closed. Clip the corner seam allowance; turn right side out. Stuff the stems firmly and sew the opening closed. Then cut a hole in the seam at the top of each fruit, insert ½ inch at one end of the stem and sew the opening closed.

5. Sew the leaf to the front with the green thread, using running stitches next to the edge.

Bring out these bright pillows and a cuddly appliquéd throw to add to the pleasures of fall spirit.

Painted Pillow

YOU WILL NEED

- pillow with a removable natural-color cover or a pillow form to make the pillow and natural-color cotton fabric to cover both sides of form, plus ½-inch seam allowance
- Decorator Blocks sponge stamps #53207 (Peaches and Pears) and Decorator Glazes in colors for apples and pears (both by Plaid Enterprises), crafts or household sponges and fabric paints
- small brush
- masking tape or clear tape
- thread (optional)
- cardboard or aluminum foil to back fabric while painting

1. Cut fabric for the pillow back and front 1 inch larger than the pillow form, or remove the cover from a purchased pillow. If not using Decorator Blocks, cut small apple and pear shapes from a dry sponge, using scissors.

2. Tape fabric for the pillow front right side out over the cardboard or foil, or insert backing inside the pillow cover.

3. Plan your design by taping tracings of the sample on the cover for placement. Then, one by one, lift the patterns, brush paint on the slightly damp sponge, and print on the fabric, *following the manufacturer's instructions.* Let the paint dry.

4. Paint stems between fruit with the small brush.

5. To complete a handmade pillow, stitch the back to the front with right sides together and ½-inch seam allowance, leaving an opening for the pillow form. Clip the seam allowance across the corners. Turn the cover right side out. Insert the form and sew the opening closed by hand.

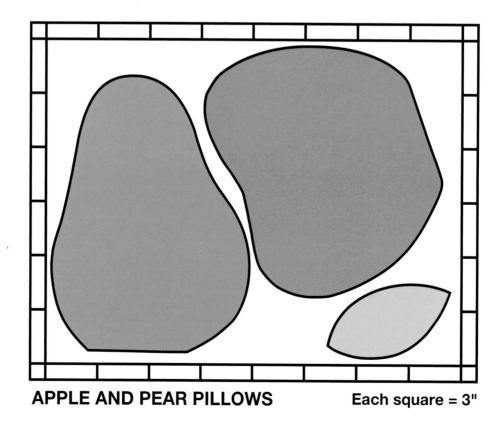

APPLE AND PEAR PILLOWS   Each square = 3"

Fleece Throw

YOU WILL NEED

- a fleece throw or thick fleece fabric, approximately 50 × 60 inches to make the throw
- ½ yard each cotton fabrics for apples, pears, and leaves
- brown and dark mustard thread for appliqués and stems
- tracing paper
- pins
- sewing machine with zigzagger
- edging for handmade throw: pearl cotton size 3 and embroidery needle to blanket-stitch or heavy sewing thread to zigzag by machine

HOW TO MAKE IT

1. To trim plain fleece, blanket-stitch by hand (see stitch diagram, below) or zigzag-stitch by machine around the edge.

2. Trace the apple, pear, and leaf patterns, below, and cut approximately 20 of each fruit and 40 leaves.

3. Alternating apples and pears, pin the fruit, without leaves, evenly spaced about 5 inches apart and 3 inches from the edge around the throw. At the top of each piece, satin-stitch a ½-inch long stem, then zigzag-stitch around the edge of the fruit.

4. Pin a leaf to each fruit and zigzag-stitch around the edge.

BLANKET STITCH

FLEECE THROW
APPLIQUE PATTERNS

Three Easy Pillows

❦ ❦ ❦

These pillows could be a first home-design project. The covers can be placed over purchased white pillow forms or over old pillows. Floral and striped fabrics look good in casual settings; also imagine using flannel or denim, velvet with satin accents, or taffeta with lace.

Bow-Tied Pillow

YOU WILL NEED

◆ 14-inch square, soft pillow form
◆ 28 × 36-inch plaid or other fabric
◆ 5 × 6-inch striped (or contrasting) fabric
◆ matching thread

HOW TO MAKE IT

1. Fold the large strip of fabric in half lengthwise, wrong side out. Stitch the long edges closed with a ½-inch seam allowance to make a tube. Fold under ½ inch twice on the open ends and topstitch ⅜ inch from the edge. Turn the tube right side out. Then stuff the pillow form into the center of the tube and set the piece aside.

2. Fold the 6-inch fabric in half lengthwise, wrong side out. With ¼-inch seam allowance, stitch one end and the long edges closed. Clip the seam allowance diagonally across the corners and turn the piece right side out. Press.

3. Pull the loose fabric on the pillow form smoothly to the front and overlap the ends. Wrap the short strip tightly around them at the center front of the pillow and fasten it behind the gathers. Arrange neat folds everywhere.

It's the little things—a bow-tied front, a smartly gathered sash, a tied-on bag—that make these three covers special.

Sash-Wrapped Pillow

YOU WILL NEED

- square 14-inch pillow form
- two 15-inch squares of fabric
- a 10 × 44-inch strip of contrasting fabric for the sash
- matching thread

HOW TO MAKE IT

1. Pin the fabric squares with their right sides together and stitch ½ inch from the edges, leaving a large opening for the pillow form on one side. Clip the seam allowance diagonally across the corners. Turn the piece right side out and insert the pillow form. Tuck in the raw edges and sew the opening closed with needle and thread.

2. Fold under 1 inch on each long edge of the 10-inch-wide strip of fabric; press. Wrap the strip around the middle of the pillow gathered slightly as a sash. Knot the ends together and tuck the raw ends into or under the knot.

Pillow in a Bag

YOU WILL NEED

- 16-inch-square pillow form
- 1 yard of 44-inch-wide fabric
- 16½-inch square of contrasting fabric
- matching thread

HOW TO MAKE IT

1. From the yard of fabric, cut a 16½ × 31-inch strip to make a bag to cover the pillow form. From leftover fabric, cut four 2 × 16-inch strips for ties.

2. Fold the large piece of fabric in half, wrong side out, with the short edges together at the top. With a ¼-inch seam allowance, stitch the sides closed to form a bag. At the opening, fold 1 inch twice to the wrong side; press. Topstitch ¾ inch from the edge. Turn the bag right side out.

3. To make the ties, press each 2 × 16-inch strip in half lengthwise, right side out. Then open the strip and press the long edges into the center. Press it in half again, enclosing the raw edges. Topstitch the folded edges closed. Pin 1 inch at one end of two ties inside the bag front, 5½ inches in from each side; pin the ends of matching ties inside the back. Knot the free end of each tie, concealing the raw ends.

4. Fold the contrasting fabric square in half, wrong side out. Stitch the short sides closed to form a bag that will be the "half cover." Fold under ½ inch on the raw edge; topstitch along the fold and turn the piece right side out.

5. Slip the half cover onto the pillow form. Then insert the pillow, uncovered end first, into the large bag. Fasten with the pairs of ties in bows at the top.

Needlepoint and Patchwork Pillow

❧ ❧ ❧

The flower is worked in half cross-stitch, a simple stitch, that both needlepoint novices and cross-stitchers can do. As a variation, the design can easily be adapted to cross-stitch on 14-count even-weave fabric, such as Aida cloth. The squares could be calicos, plaids, satins, or velvets, and the piping and welting are optional.

SIZE

16 inches square

YOU WILL NEED

- 8-inch square of 14-count natural color linen mono canvas
- 1 skein each DMC Floralia 3-ply Persian Wool: white; yellow 7579, dark yellow 7712, tan 7381, peach 7484, and orange 7485
- 1 yard DMC Six-Strand Embroidery Floss, yellow 307
- tapestry, embroidery, and sewing needles
- 6-inch-square black cotton fabric
- ¼ yard each natural and red linen (or other fabrics) for patches
- natural color thread
- 24 inches of ¼-inch-diameter piping cord
- ¼ yard of red pin-dot fabric to cover the piping cord on the bias
- 2 yards of 1-inch-diameter welting cord
- ¼ yard of natural-and-red vertically striped fabric (or 1 yard horizontally striped) to cover the welting cord

As fresh as a daisy, this patchwork design in crisp linen has plump striped welting and a bright needlepoint centerpiece.

- 16-inch-square fabric for the pillow back
- 16-inch-square, knife-edge pillow form
- masking tape
- sewing machine with zipper foot

HOW TO MAKE IT

Needlepoint: **1.** Fold masking tape over the canvas edges to prevent raveling. Mark the horizontal and vertical center lines with basting stitches. Outline with basting or pencil a 5-inch square centered on the canvas and following the mesh lines.

2. Separate the yarn into 18-inch lengths of two strands and thread the tapestry needle. Centering the design in the square, work the daisy in half cross-stitch (see the stitch diagram following the design chart, opposite. Each square on the chart equals one stitch or one mesh thread. Enclose the yarn ends on the back under the stitches and trim them.

3. Divide the six-strand floss to use three 18-inch strands and embroider X's around the flower center at random, crossing each one in the same direction.

4. Place the canvas facedown on a towel and steam-press it lightly to flatten and straighten it if necessary.

5. Baste the black fabric to the back of the canvas, sewing along the marked outline.

6. *Piping:* Cut two or more 2-inch-wide strips of dotted fabric on the bias. (To cut bias strips: Fold fabric end down even with one side edge and cut strips parallel to the diagonal fold created.) Sew the strips together end to end to measure 24 inches. Pin the strip right side out over the 1/4-inch-thick cord. Using the zipper foot on your machine, stitch close to the cord. Pin the welt around the square, just inside the outline, with the raw edges outward. Overlap the ends and cut diagonally. Baste along the outline.

Pillow: **1.** Cut four 6-inch squares each from the red and natural fabrics. On the wrong side, mark stitching lines 1/2 inch in from the edges, to outline 5-inch squares.

2. With the right sides together, stitch the fabric and needlepoint squares into strips of three, following the photograph for placement. Stitch the strips together to form a square.

3. Cut two 3-inch-wide strips across the vertically striped fabric (or lengthwise from the horizontally striped) so stripes run across the strips. Stitch the strips end to end to make one long strip, keeping the continuity of the stripe pattern. Fold, pin, and stitch the strip right side out over the welting cord.

4. Mark a 15-inch square centered on the wrong side of the patchwork for the stitching line. Inserting pins from the back, pin the welting, with the raw edge outward and the welt just inside the line, to the front of the patchwork, rounding the corners. To join the ends, push back the fabric, overlap the cord ends and cut them to butt. Then tack the ends together. Lap one end of the fabric over the other, turn under the raw edge, and sew it in place. Sewing between the welt and the welt seam, baste the welt to the stitching line.

5. *Finishing:* Pin the back fabric to the patchwork with the right sides together. Stitch along the basted line, leaving an opening for stuffing. Turn the cover right side out. Insert the pillow form. Tuck in the raw edges and sew the opening closed by hand. Remove the basting.

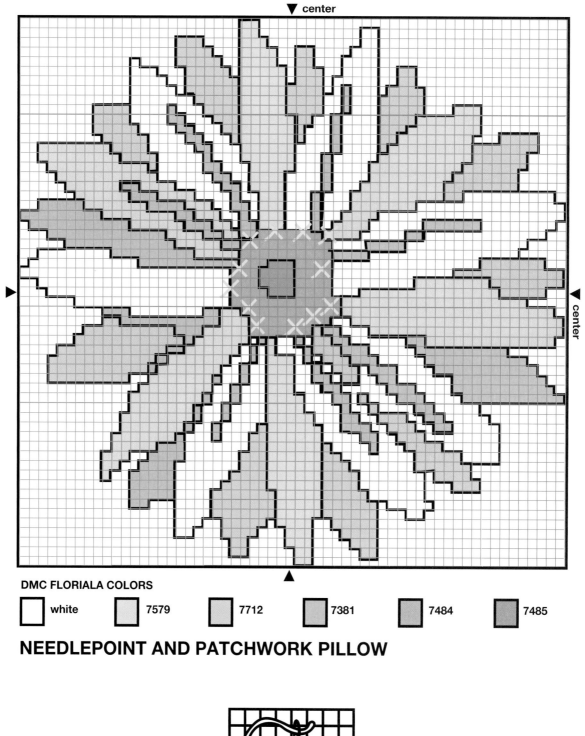

center

center

DMC FLORIALA COLORS

☐ white ▨ 7579 ▨ 7712 ▨ 7381 ▨ 7484 ▨ 7485

NEEDLEPOINT AND PATCHWORK PILLOW

HALF CROSS-STITCH

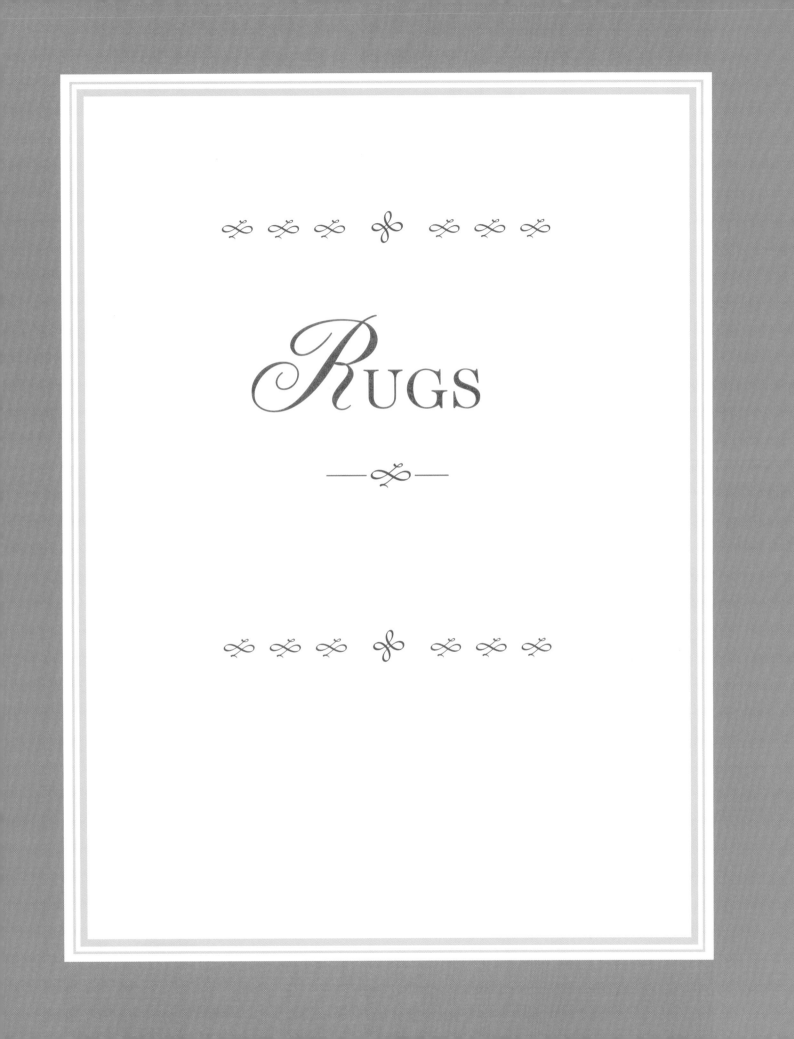

RUGS

You don't need special skills to make this rug, but it requires a fair amount of time. (Worth it, for a hand-made showpiece.)

Flower-Stenciled Rug

✤ ✤ ✤

Once you've laid out and painted the border, the flowers are a breeze to do with simple stencils you cut. If you hate to make straight lines, you can paint a single band of color for the border and omit the checks. It's the technique of rug painting that counts here and you can adapt it to your needs and color scheme.

YOU WILL NEED

- flat-woven, natural-color cotton rug about 31 × 44 inches
- 2-oz bottles of acrylic paint (Plaid Enterprises' FolkArt Acrylic Colors Lemonade, French Blue, Hot Pink, Wicker White, Poetry Green, Baby Pink, and Yellow Ochre Artists' Pigment)
- 6 oz of FolkArt Textile Medium
- two 25 × 40-inch sheets of matte acetate or waxed stencil paper for stencils
- stencil knife or small sharp scissors
- spray adhesive (or stencil adhesive)
- 1-inch-wide masking tape
- water-soluble fabric marker
- yardstick
- clear plastic ruler
- fine-point permanent black or blue marker
- ½-inch and 1-inch stencil brushes
- medium-size round paintbrush
- small mixing pans with lids or plastic wrap
- plastic drop cloth
- tracing paper
- tablespoon
- clean rag

HOW TO MAKE IT

1. Use the full-size flower patterns, page 105, or trace flowers from fabric in your room to use as coordinating patterns.

2. Allowing a 1½-inch border around each stencil, trace the flowers, leaves, and centers separately onto acetate or stencil paper with the permanent marker.

3. Cut out the shapes with the knife or scissors, leaving the margins intact (see *Stenciling Basics*, page 177). Spray the back of the stencils with adhesive and let it dry.

4. Tape a drop cloth to your worktable and spread the rug on top. Referring to the Border Diagram, below, with the fabric marker and yardstick, outline a 28¾ × 43-inch rectangle centered on the rug (or outline close to the edge if your rug is a different size, allowing for ¾-inch squares in the gingham border).

5. Outline the pink stripes and blue grid of ¾-inch squares for the border on the rug using the *fabric* marker. Then cut separate stencils of three or more rows each for light blue and dark blue squares according to repeats on the diagram. Mask the outer edges of the pink border stripes with tape. (Protect other areas of the rug with paper.)

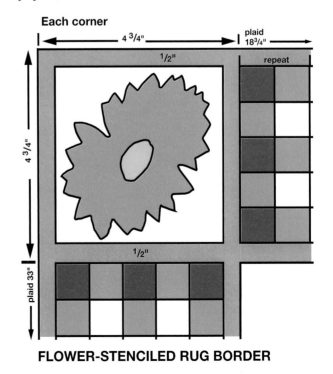

FLOWER-STENCILED RUG BORDER

6. *Pink border:* Mix 2 tablespoons of Hot Pink paint with 1 tablespoon textile medium. Work the paint onto the rug by dabbing it on with the stencil brush. Let the paint dry; remove the tape.

7. *Blue border:* For the light blue squares, mix 2 tablespoons of white paint with 1 tablespoon French Blue and 1½ tablespoons textile medium. Stencil the light blue squares. (Overlap a row of squares on the previous print to make repeats.) When dry, mix blue paint with textile medium and stencil the darker blue squares.

8. *Flowers:* Trace the flower stencils onto the rug with the fabric marker, placing a blue flower in the corner squares facing the center and blue and yellow flowers evenly spaced at random throughout. (To prearrange the design, make many photocopies of the patterns, color them, and arrange them on the rug before marking.) Fill in with groups of pink flowers. Add leaves to some flowers.

9. To paint the flowers, use one color at a time mixed 2 parts color to 1 part textile medium, *following the manufacturer's directions.* Stencil the base color of the flower (see suggested colors below) and let it dry. Stencil the centers, then brush a darker color in from the edges to shade the petals. Stencil green leaves. With the round brush, partly outline the centers in green.

Suggested flower colors: Blue flowers: Mix 1 part French Blue with 2 parts white for the base. Paint the centers Lemonade. Shade the petals with unmixed blue. Add a dot of Baby Pink to the center. *Yellow flowers:* Paint with Lemonade and shade with Yellow Ochre. Stencil green leaf/stems. *Pink flowers:* Paint Baby Pink with Lemonade centers. Shade with Hot Pink. Stencil green leaves. Stroke green around the centers with the round brush.

10. Let the paint dry for 24 hours. Then lightly dab off any visible marker lines with a damp sponge. For extra durability, heat-set the paint, *following the textile-medium instructions.*

FLOWER-STENCILED RUG

Crocheted Rag Rug

❧ ❧ ❧

The fabrics are cut or torn into strips. A rotary cutter and mat can make quick work of this step and you can cut several layers at once. As you crochet, you don't have to fold or twist the fabric, just let the strip gather naturally. And the finished product is reversible: one side is smooth, the other framed in raised single-crochet borders.

SIZE

26 × 34 inches, which is easily made larger by adding squares.

YOU WILL NEED

- fabric: ¾ yard each of twelve 44-inch-wide cotton or cotton-blend blue prints (or any other colors). For extra squares, ¾ yard each.
- an extra ½ yard of a dark and a medium blue to have enough fabric for borders and seams
- wood or metal crochet hook size N (10.00 mm)
- scissors or a rotary fabric cutter and mat
- ruler

HOW TO MAKE IT

Note: Crochet abbreviations used are listed on page 173.

1. Cut ½-inch-wide strips across the fabric. With right sides together, stitch strips of same color together about ⅛ inch from the ends to form one long strip of each color. Wind the strips into balls. (*Note:* The fabric can also be cut in one continuous strip by stopping ½ inch before each side and cutting the next row ½ inch below in the opposite direction; this forms wide sections on the strip, but they can be gathered in as you crochet.)

2. With crochet hook and a fabric strip, chain 16 stitches loosely or enough stitches to make an 8-inch-long chain.

Row 1: Sc in the second ch from the hook and in each ch across. Mark this row with a safety pin for the right side of the work.

Row 2: Ch 1, turn. Sc in each stitch across. Repeat Row 2 until you have an 8-inch square. Fasten off. Make 12 squares, measuring each against the first square to make all the same size.

3. Lay out the squares right side up in four rows of three, alternating the direction of the crocheted rows. To join them, hold two squares back to back. With medium blue fabric, sc the edges together, making four strips of three squares and spacing the stitches to keep the edge flat. (If you run out of one color, continue with another.) Then sc the four strips together to form the rug. Conceal the ends neatly so that the raised grid formed by the joinings will look good on the front of the rug (see detail, below).

4. *Border:* With a dark color, sc around the outer edge, working 3 sts in each corner. Join with a slip stitch in the first st. Fasten off.

THE OTHER SIDE

You're in luck if you save leftovers from sewing projects and know two basic crochet stitches, because a dozen three-quarter-yard cotton prints and a fat crochet hook are all it takes to produce this handsome rug.

"Tiled" Floorcloth

The secret of making this great little area rug is to cut colored papers with bravery and abandon. You want the irregularity to be part of the look. So slice away. Then just glue the cutouts to a canvas base and varnish the surface.

YOU WILL NEED

- **24 × 38-inch rectangle of primed artist's canvas**
- **light blue and burnt umber acrylic paint**
- **large sheet each of dark blue, red, yellow, and white construction paper**
- **Mod Podge sealer/glue**
- **tacky glue or a glue gun and glue sticks**
- **1-inch and 2-inch foam or bristle paintbrushes**
- **clear varnish**
- **masking tape**
- **scissors**

HOW TO MAKE IT

1. Spread out the canvas, wrong side up, on a work surface protected with paper or plastic. Before you mark the hem, check for square corners by measuring diagonally from upper to opposite corners; the measurements should be the same. If not, mark where they would be the same and trim the canvas.

2. On the wrong side of the canvas, with ruler and pencil, mark a hemline 1 inch in from the edges. Cut away excess at the corners diagonally so you can fold mitered corners. Then fold the 1-inch-wide hem to the wrong side on the line and glue it to the back with the tacky glue or hot glue. Weight the edge with books or magazines to crease the edge firmly until the glue dries.

3. Turn the canvas over and tint the front with a coat of water-thinned blue paint. Let dry.

4. To make a design, cut papers freehand into shapes and arrange them about 3/8 inch apart on the canvas. Or follow the photograph to copy our design like this: Cut long blue paper strips freehand, about 1 3/4 inches wide. Cut these strips into varied 1- to 4-inch lengths and space them about 3/8 inch apart near the edge of the canvas to form a border. Place a border of 3 1/2-inch-wide yellow patches next. Then draw and cut a double spiral from red paper to fit the center. Fill the remaining space with patches of white paper.

5. To attach papers, outline their positions lightly in pencil on the canvas. Remove the papers to a clean area on one side, keeping them more or less in position. One at a time, brush Mod Podge on both the rug and the back of the paper and put the paper in place with your hand. Then brush Mod Podge over the front of the papers as you smooth them in place. Let the glue dry.

6. To antique the surface, thin burnt umber paint with an equal amount of water. Brush it on the rug and, while it is still wet, wipe it off with a clean rag. Let the the paint dry.

7. Apply two or three coats of varnish to make the rug sturdy and waterproof, following the manufacturer's directions for application and drying.

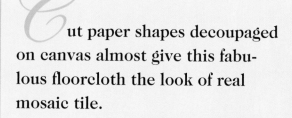

Cut paper shapes decoupaged on canvas almost give this fabulous floorcloth the look of real mosaic tile.

Fruit-Stenciled Rug

✥ ✥ ✥

A flat-woven rug can usually be found at a housewares-import store. Handpainted or stenciled designs are then directly applied with acrylic or fabric paints.

YOU WILL NEED

- a white flat-woven fabric rug 30 × 46 inches or slightly larger
- acrylic paints (Plaid Enterprises' FolkArt Acrylic Colors 2-oz bottle each Autumn Leaves, Cardinal Red, Fresh Foliage, Kelly Green, Licorice, Shamrock, and FolkArt Artists' Pigments Cobalt, Yellow Ochre, and Yellow Light)
- 6 oz of FolkArt Textile Medium
- 2¼ yards of self-stick vinyl (such as Con-Tact)
- roll of shelf paper
- three 9 × 12-inch sheets of matte acetate for stencils
- ½-inch and ¾-inch stencil brushes
- permanent black marker
- masking tape
- yardstick
- large jar
- paint pan
- fine scissors or craft knife
- transfer paper
- optional: graph paper and large sheets of tracing paper for pattern

*G*ive a plain rug personality with stenciled designs and latticework.

1. Enlarge the quarter rug pattern, at right (see *How to Enlarge Patterns*, page174). Trace the enlarged pattern and tape the halves together, or tape two photocopies together, to make a *half pattern*. (Or make a pattern for a design of your own that has simple shapes to stencil.)

2. Transfer the design to the rug with transfer paper (transfer half the design, then rotate the pattern and match the center lines to trace the second half). Transfer the lattice pattern to the back of self-stick plastic to make masks for the diamond shapes.

3. *Cut the stencils:* Tape a square of acetate over one apple pattern and trace the outline with the marker (omit the black dots on the fruit). Repeat for the other apple, fruit, and leaves. Cut out the shapes with scissors or a craft knife, leaving the background intact. (See also *Stenciling Basics*, page 177.) Set aside.

4. *Mask the straight lines:* Apply masking tape along the edges of the rectangular borders. Cut masks for the spaces in the lattice from self-stick plastic. Peel off the paper backing and press the masks in place on the rug. Protect the band of fruit with shelving paper.

5. *Paint the borders:* Pour the bottle of Cobalt paint into the large jar and stir in 1 ounce of textile medium. Pour a small amount of the mixture into the paint pan. Dip in the stencil brush, blot it on paper or on the pan, then work the paint into the rug with a dabbing motion. Let the paint dry (a hair dryer can be used to speed this up). Remove the masks and tape.

6. *Stencil the fruit:* Using one color at a time, mix 1 part textile medium to 2 parts color. Tape

FRUIT-STENCILED RUG QUARTER PATTERN

the fruit stencil in position on the border (protect surroundings). Dab on color, working from the edges in. Lift the stencil before the paint dries and wipe off the wet paint so you can flop the stencil as needed. Let the paint dry.

7. *Add the details:* With the small brush, paint black dots and stems. Set the paint, *following the manufacturer's directions.*

Painted Straw Rug

❧ ❧ ❧

Straw, maize, and other natural fiber rugs are available in most housewares-import stores, and these rugs are not expensive. They're especially soothing summer rugs and in warm areas can be used all year round. The paint can be bright or subtle, adding a touch of color that unifies the room.

YOU WILL NEED

- ◆ natural fiber rug with a square pattern
- ◆ 2 colors of acrylic paint
- ◆ 2 foam paintbrushes
- ◆ jars for paint
- ◆ masking tape

A wonderful way to give a classic a lift for one of the best summery and casual looks against a sleek hardwood floor.

HOW TO MAKE IT

1. Thin the paint with water to a milky consistency. (Test the coverage on the back of the rug and rebalance the proportions if the paint appears too thin. Refer to the photograph for the effect.)

2. Mask the edges of the small center square of each square on the rug if you like. Paint the small square with the lighter color. (If the paint drips, wipe it up with a wet rag or sponge immediately to prevent stains.) Let the paint dry and remove the tape.

3. Paint a border of the darker color, about four woven rows wide, around each square.

HOLDERS

Rope-Hung Shelves

❧ ❧ ❧

Hang one shelf or a tier of two or three. Spacing is up to you, but for satisfactory results keep the span short and make sure the ropes are anchored securely. To hang the shower curtain, simply wind rope through the curtain holes and over the shower rod, as shown in the photograph. To tie the curtain, glue a few shells to a rope about 30 inches long; wrap and tie it loosely around the middle.

Hoist some handy shelves with rope for a great natural look in the bathroom. Pair it with a rope-hung-and-tied shower curtain.

HOW TO MAKE IT

1. Sand the edges of the shelf to round them. Dust off the residue with the tack cloth. Brush on two coats of polyurethane (or paint), *following the manufacturer's instructions.*

2. Mark the wall lightly with pencil and ruler to indicate the placement of the shelf. Note that each shelf is hung from a separate pair of hooks. The hooks should be centered above the shelf, about 2 inches from each end of the shelf and about 16 inches apart (possibly aligned over studs in the wall for stability). Place at least one hook about 16 inches above the shelf. The hooks do not have to be at the same height, but make any difference count visually, as in the photograph.

3. Install the hooks. Wrap tape around one end of the rope to prevent raveling. Attach this end firmly to the back edge of the shelf, 2 inches in from the end, with one or two furniture tacks.

4. With a helper holding the shelf, loop the rope over the hook above, to the front of the shelf, under it, and up the back edge. Mark the rope at the proper length. Remove the shelf and rope from the wall; trim and tape the end and tack it to the back edge of the shelf next to the other end.

5. Install the other rope in the same way, checking to make sure the shelf is straight by placing the level on top.

Twine and Paper Canisters

❧ ❧ ❧

All it takes is corrugated paper, twine, spray adhesive, and tacky glue to recycle handsomely.

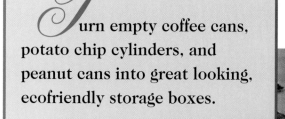

*T*urn empty coffee cans, potato chip cylinders, and peanut cans into great looking, ecofriendly storage boxes.

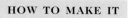

HOW TO MAKE IT

1. Remove the labels and wash and dry the containers well.

2. Measure the height and circumference of the can and cut corrugated paper to fit. Apply spray adhesive to the back of the paper and the outside of the can. Align the top of the paper with the upper edge of the can and attach it carefully little by little.

3. Trace the lid onto posterboard or bristol board. Cut out the shape and glue it to the top of the lid with tacky glue or hot glue. Then cut a 1-inch- or ⅜-inch-wide strip of the same material long enough to fit around the side of the lid. Glue the strip around the lid, flush at the top.

4. Starting at the center of the top and working out in a spiral pattern, glue the twine to the top, then the side of the lid using tacky glue applied a little at a time (thin the glue with water if necessary).

5. Starting at the lower edge of the container and working upward, wind and glue a band of twine the same size as the lid band around the side of the container.

6. Print a label on brown paper, cut it out, and glue it to the front of the canister. Glue twine around the edge.

*A*ll that glitters need not be gold, and the bathroom or bedroom are good places for some indulgence in colored baubles.

Jeweled Cup and *Mirror*

✣ ✣ ✣

YOU WILL NEED

◆ glassware (mirror, cup, vase, or frame)
◆ colored balls for floral arranging or acrylic jewels (from florist and crafts stores)
◆ glue gun

HOW TO MAKE THEM

1. Plan the spacing and color arrangement by taping the balls temporarily in place.

2. Remove one at a time. Place a daub of hot glue on the bauble, then stick the bauble to the glass and hold it in place until it adheres. (It will adhere quickly.)

Stacked Boxes

❧ ❧ ❧

Boxes in graduated sizes of wood or cardboard are available in most crafts stores. Painted, they become decorative as well as practical storage places for gloves, hats, games, ornaments, sewing notions, rubber bands, and so on. When not in use, they nestle nicely to save space. The ones shown in the illustration are potato printed, but you can sponge print, stencil, or paint flat colors to equally good effect.

*S*torage and craft go hand in hand with these classic boxes. Relive childhood to stamp each one with different potato prints and stack them high for a wonderful, colorful note almost anywhere.

- round or oval wooden or cardboard boxes (the diameters of the six boxes shown are 5½, 7½, 9½, 11½, 13½, and 15½ inches respectively)
- assorted acrylic paints (we used red, yellow, blue, and green)
- burnt umber acrylic paint to antique the surface
- medium-size potatoes
- a clean, lint-free rag
- household sponge
- paper scraps for patterns
- sharp kitchen knife
- plastic plates for paint
- clear acrylic finish

HOW TO MAKE IT

1. Plan a color scheme by rotating colors throughout the stack. (Make small swatches to remind you.) Have a color major on one, minor on the next, and so on.

2. Remove the lids to paint them separately. Wipe the selected background colors on the boxes and lids with the rag or sponge. For a stained background as shown, thin the color about 1 to 1 with water (test the coverage on the box bottom and adjust it if necessary).

3. Draw or trace small motifs to print on the boxes and cut a paper pattern for each one. These can be diamonds, clubs, flowers, squares, chevrons, and so on, as in the photograph. Lightly mark the desired placement on the sides of the box and lid. (Tip: For even placement, measure the box's circumference and divide it by twice the width of the motif. For example, if the motif is 1½ inches wide, divide the circumference by 3. Start and end at the back seam, if there is one, and adjust any uneven spacing there.)

4. Wash and dry the potatoes. Cutting each in half as needed, blot the flesh on a paper towel. Then place the pattern on the cut surface and trace around it with the knife or pencil. Remove the pattern and cut away the surrounding potato about ¼ inch deep.

5. To print, pour the paint onto a plate, press the potato into the paint (or brush the paint onto the potato). Holding the box firmly, gently stamp the design on the side. You'll get one or two prints from each paint application. After the print dries, you can touch it up with a brush if necessary. Print all the designs and let the paint dry.

6. To antique the surface, apply a 1 to 1 water-thinned coat of burnt umber and wipe it off while wet with a clean, lint-free rag.

7. Spray with a clear acrylic finish.

Small Shelf Five Ways

❧ ❧ ❧

Small places are where you can indulge some whimsy. If you're daunted by hammers and saws and don't want to build the shelf, refresh an old shelf or buy unfinished new ones for these projects.

YOU WILL NEED

- 25-inch length of 1 × 8 pine lumber for a 7½ × 20-inch shelf as shown, or lumber for the length of shelf you want plus 5 inches for brackets (add a center bracket if the shelf will be longer than 36 inches)
- ruler
- pencil
- four 2-inch finishing nails
- wood glue
- wood putty or natural filler if staining
- fine sandpaper on a wood block
- clear water-base or polyurethane finish
- synthetic or foam paintbrushes
- nail set
- hammer
- saw
- 2 sawtooth or loop hangers
- 2 nails or screws and anchors for your type of wall
- primer and acrylic paint for solid color or acrylic paint alone for a color stain
- clear finish

HOW TO MAKE IT

1. Mark the wood with the ruler and pencil as in the cutting diagram, opposite. Then hold or clamp the wood firmly on the work surface and cut the shelf and two brackets with the saw.

2. Mark the top and bottom across the shelf for brackets 2 inches in from each end, as shown in the nailing diagram, below. (Place brackets further in on any shelves longer than 22 inches). Look at the end grain of your wood. The convex curve should be at the top.

3. In the upper marked area, insert two evenly spaced nails until the tips show on the underside. Glue the bracket to the underside and finish nailing. Let the glue dry.

4. Sink the nailheads by placing the nail set over each one and tapping it with the hammer. If you're going to paint the shelf, fill the resulting small holes with putty (apply it with a nailhead). If you will be applying a clear or stained finish, use filler that matches the wood. Let the putty or filler dry.

5. Sand the top and edges, following the wood grain. Dust off the residue.

6. To paint the shelf a solid color, apply a white primer. Let it dry. Then brush on two or more coats of paint, letting each one dry. To stain the shelf, apply a woodstain or acrylic paint thinned with an equal amount of water.

7. Apply clear finish over paint, stain, or unfinished wood, *following the manufacturer's directions.*

8. Attach hangers to the shelf behind the brackets. Find the wall studs if possible (16 inches apart) and use nails to hang the shelf, or use screws and anchors. To make sure the shelf is level, hang one side. Place a carpenter's level (or a ball) on the shelf. When the liquid is level (or the ball stops rolling), mark the wall and hang the other side.

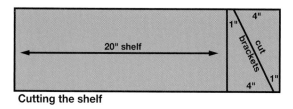

Cutting the shelf

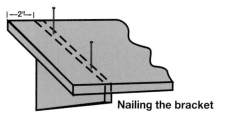

Nailing the bracket

SMALL SHELF FIVE WAYS

PLEATS AND BUTTONS

THE TRIMS

Pleats and Buttons:

1. Paint the shelf white.

2. Measure the front and sides of the shelf and buy 1½ times this length of 3-inch-wide gingham or other ribbon for the pleated edging. Then mark the edge of shelf every 2½ inches for pleats.

3. With a staple gun, attach one end of the ribbon to the left back corner of the shelf. To fold pleats, staple the ribbon to the shelf at the next 2½-inch mark. Fold it back and staple ⅝ inch from the fold. Fold it forward to the next mark; staple and pleat as before. Continue along the shelf and staple the end to the right-back corner.

4. Attach a button over each pleat with a glue gun (nip off any shanks with old scissors or wire snips). Or insert a decorative furniture tack over each pleat.

The basic wall shelf is an absolute breeze to make. Once it's built, give it one of these lively touches, or invent your own.

Twine:

1. Paint the shelf blue or finish it as you like.

2. Measure the front and side edges of the shelf and add 2 inches. Cut two strips of ¼-inch-thick sisal twine this length.

3. Working on a protected surface (waxed paper or aluminum foil), lightly glue the twine strips side by side with a glue gun or tacky glue. Let the glue dry.

4. Wrap jute twine around the sisal pair every 2 inches or so and glue the ends to one side for the back.

5. Finally, glue the assembled twine to the edge of the shelf. Trim any excess length.

TWINE

Seashells:

1. Apply a clear polyurethane finish to the shelf, or stain the shelf with water-thinned white acrylic paint. Hang the shelf on the wall, or at least prepare its location with nails or screws to keep from damaging the shells when you hang the shelf.

2. Attach seashells from your collection (or cockle and snail shells purchased at a crafts or shell store) to the edge of the shelf, using a hot-glue gun.

SEASHELLS

Lace:

1. Paint or stain the shelf white.

2. With a low-temperature glue gun attach 1½-inch-wide lace trim along the edge.

LACE

Tacks and Checks:

1. Paint the shelf top white. Let the paint dry.

2. With a pencil and ruler, mark off squares as evenly as possible (1⅞ × 2 inches on a 7½ × 20-inch shelf).

3. Cover every other square with masking tape, pressing the edges down firmly.

4. Paint the alternate squares red, as many coats as needed to cover, letting each coat dry. Remove the tape.

5. Paint the edge of the shelf black, one bracket bright yellow and the other bright blue.

6. Press ⅜-inch-diameter red furniture tacks 1 inch apart into the edges.

TACKS AND CHECKS

ACCENTS

Autumn Plate and Candle Holders

❧ ❧ ❧

You'll need to photocopy the leaves for the decoupage plate, but you can decorate the candle holders with real leaves.

Gilded and Decoupaged Plate

- 10-inch (or any other size) clean glass plate (ours has an optional gold edge)
- 1 large and 8 small fall leaves
- access to a color photocopier
- matte decoupage sealer/glue
- Dutch Metal gold leaf
- black or dark green acrylic paint
- small sharp scissors
- flat 1-inch paintbrush
- china marker
- waxed paper or aluminum foil

Note: For this project the glass should be as clean as possible. After washing and drying it, rub it with alcohol to remove any grease.

Capture the beauty of fall leaves at their brightest and enjoy them all year long.

1. Photocopy the leaves in color. For best results when tracing, photocopying, or gluing, the leaves should be smooth and flat. Press them between the pages of a phone book or in a flower press for a day or two if necessary. To photocopy, place the leaf facedown on the color copier and cover it with white paper, then make the print.

2. Cut out the paper copies neatly above their edges, then arrange them on the front of the plate. Lightly outline the placement with the china marker. Remove the leaves.

3. Lay out the paper leaves on waxed paper or aluminum foil. One at a time, brush a thin coat of sealer/glue on the *front* of the leaf. Don't leave any gaps and work out to all the edges. Add a thin coat of glue to the *back* of the glass in the leaf's position, then smooth the leaf in place with your fingers. Press out from the center to remove any air bubbles. Let the glue dry.

4. Brush glue over the back of the plate and leaves and lay on sheets of gold Dutch Metal, *following the manufacturer's directions.* The sheets may break up, but this crackling is part of the look. When the glue has dried, remove any flaking gold leaf with a soft brush.

5. Seal the back of the plate with a coat of glue. Let the glue dry.

6. Paint one coat of black or dark green color on the back of the plate. When this is dry, apply two coats of glue, letting each coat dry. Rub marker lines off the front with a cloth or a paper towel.

Candle Holder

- a candle in a tall glass holder (available in supermarkets), or a small votive holder and candle
- small amounts of thin white rice paper
- green, yellow, and orange tissue paper
- small pressed leaves
- matte decoupage sealer/glue
- small flat paintbrush
- waxed paper or aluminum foil

Note: Pick up the leaves before they are completely dry and flatten them in a phone book or flower press.

1. Wash and dry the outside of the glass. A final rub with alcohol will remove any remaining grease.

2. Tear small, irregular shapes from the rice paper and colored tissue.

3. Brush glue on the outside of the glass and pat a thin layer of assorted papers in place with your fingers or the glue brush, letting the edges overlap and gluing down overlapped edges. Cover the outside completely and let the glue dry.

4. Glue leaves at random to the paper-covered glass as follows: Place the leaves facedown on waxed paper or aluminum foil. One at a time, brush a thin coat of glue on the *back* and apply a little glue in the leaf's intended position on the glass. Lift the leaf by its edges (or use tweezers so you don't rub glue off) and smooth it in place with your fingers or the glue brush. Let the glue dry.

5. Add more torn papers, some overlapping the leaves, to vary the luminosity.

6. Apply two thin coats of glue as a finish, *following the manufacturer's directions.*

Fishing-Pole Mirror

No, they're not your old fishing poles, but with a few strands of thread and a few floats, they look like it. You could build a similar frame with twigs or dowels.

YOU WILL NEED

- an old mirror
- bamboo poles (from a florist or garden center): 8 cut 5 inches longer than the mirror's length and 8 cut 5 inches longer than the mirror's width
- red, black, green, and blue embroidery floss, string, or thread
- 6 yards of jute twine
- 2 small plastic floats
- a few inches of fish line
- glue gun

HOW TO MAKE IT

1. Wind and glue the floss, thread, or string around the poles, making ½- to 1-inch-long bands at random intervals.

2. To make the frame, lay out four poles side by side, centered lengthwise over the two long edges of the mirror. Glue the poles side by side, but not to the mirror. Glue four poles each across these to lie over the short edges. Tie a yard of twine in an X around each corner.

3. Firmly attach the bamboo frame to the mirror frame with the glue gun. Tie the floats to alternate corners with the fishline.

A few bamboo poles give new life to an old mirror, and it is a great catch for a porch or outdoor shower.

Stone-like texture gives a purchased frame a serene rustic air.

Stone-Painted Frame

❧ ❧ ❧

Coat a new, unfinished wood frame or revive an old one with a flecked spray paint. This finish can unify a group of framed photographs or prints displayed together.

YOU WILL NEED

- a flat wooden frame
- ¼-inch-thick plywood square for each corner (optional)

- two shades of Fleck Stone textured spray paint by Plasti-Kote
- acrylic paint and brushes for the undercoat (optional)
- newspapers or plastic to protect work surfaces
- glue gun for the squares
- scrap wood or cardboard to practice painting

HOW TO MAKE IT

Paint the frame one color and the squares another, *following the paint manufacturer's instructions.* When the paint is dry, glue the squares to the frame.

Striped Frames

✤ ✤ ✤

Even if the background of your room is conservative, you can have fun with the details. After all, you can always change them. And these frames are covered with nothing more than paint, torn rice paper, and a few fabric scraps.

YOU WILL NEED

- unfinished wooden frame for a 5 × 7-inch picture
- dried naturals to display
- 1-inch foam paintbrush
- fine sandpaper
- corrugated cardboard for backing
- 2 thumbtacks or screw eyes
- wire or string for hanging
- glue gun
- *painted stripes:* yellow, periwinkle, and white acrylic paint; round and liner paintbrushes
- *fabric stripes:* yellow acrylic paint; blue polka-dot fabric; pinking shears; matte decoupage glue (Mod Podge)
- *paper stripes:* white acrylic paint; light blue and dark blue rice paper; matte decoupage glue

HOW TO MAKE THEM

Painted Stripes: **1.** Paint the frame two coats of periwinkle with the flat brush.

2. When the paint is dry, with the round brush make wavy yellow stripes about 1¼ inches apart across the frame. With the liner brush, paint a fine white line between the yellow stripes.

Fabric Stripes: **1.** Paint the frame yellow. Let the paint dry, then sand it lightly to let some wood show through.

2. Cut long ¾-inch-wide strips of fabric with pinking shears for stripes. Pencil diagonal guidelines on the frame about 2 inches apart.

3. Brush decoupage glue over the lines and smooth the fabric on. The strips should cover the side and center edges of the frame as well as the front. Brush glue on as a finish. Let the glue dry. Trim the ends even with the frame.

Paper Stripes: **1.** Brush one coat of white paint onto the frame and sand it lightly when the paint is dry.

2. Crease and tear 1¼-inch-wide strips of light blue paper to fit lengthwise on the frame, including the center and side edges. Glue the strips to the frame, spaced fairly evenly, and trim the ends.

3. Cut fourteen 1 × ¾-inch patches of dark blue paper. Glue and seal the rectangles diagonally onto the blue strips as shown.

Finishing, All Frames: Hot-glue cardboard to the back of the frame. Attach string or wire for hanging with tacks or eyelets. Glue a spray of dried flowers or grasses, tied with string or fabric, to the front.

These jazzy frames in pretty striped themes are an exciting complement to the delicate flowers inside.

Five Country Shades

❧ ❧ ❧

Most of these lampshades are easily done by gluing, cutting, or tying natural materials onto plain paper or fabric-covered plastic shades. The naturals add interest in both modern and country settings.

Shells and Raffia

YOU WILL NEED

- paper or plastic-backed-fabric lampshade
- small seashells
- raffia

- hole punch
- drill with extra-fine (1/16-inch) bit
- fish line
- glue gun or tacky glue
- scrap wood

HOW TO MAKE IT

1. Punch a row of holes about 1 inch apart and ½ inch from the top and bottom edges of the lampshade.

2. Prepare a shell for every second hole at the upper edge: Hold the shell firmly on the scrap wood and drill a hole near the base. Thread a short strand of fish line through the hole and tie a loop; secure the knot with a drop of glue.

3. Following the photograph, wrap a few strands of raffia through the holes and over the upper edge. String a shell on the strands at the front of every second hole. Glue the raffia ends inside the shade.

4. For the lower edge, twist together long strands of raffia to form a ½-inch-thick "rope." Glue the rope around the lower edge, then wrap it in place with two strands of raffia threaded through the punched holes and over the edge, adding shells at intervals as you go.

Cutwork

YOU WILL NEED

- paper or plastic-backed-fabric shade
- craft knife

With a few minutes and with raffia, stencils, or a few leaves, you can trim the light fantastically. And the special effects don't stop there!

1. Determine how many 1½-inch squares will fit evenly spaced on your paper shade, and mark the four corners of each with pencil. Lightly connect the dots to form an X in each square.

2. Cut along the X with a sharp craft knife. Carefully fold back each triangle to create a creased square, leaving open slits for the light to shine through.

Burlap Pleats

◆ pleated paper shade
◆ burlap
◆ raffia
◆ white glue

1. Cut the shade open along the seam. Lay the shade flat, brush glue on the outside (thin the glue with water if necessary), and cover it with burlap. When the glue is dry, trim the burlap edges to match the shade. Glue the seam closed.

2. With a sharp pointed tool or large needle, punch a hole through the two layers of each pleat about ½ inch from the upper edge. Thread two strands of raffia through the holes, gather the top, and tie a knot. Tie a bow of raffia over the knot.

Leaves

◆ paper shade
◆ small leaves
◆ decoupage sealer/glue
◆ small paintbrush
◆ tweezers

1. Press leaves flat in a flower press or between the pages of a phone book for a day or two. Don't let them get too dry.

2. Lightly mark the placement of the leaves on the shade with pencil. With tweezers, dip the leaves into the decoupage sealer/glue (or brush glue on the backs), and arrange them on the shade. Let the glue dry.

3. Seal the leaves with one or two coats of glue, *following the manufacturer's instructions*.

Stencils

◆ paper or fabric shade
◆ small stencil or blank stencil paper
◆ craft knife
◆ acrylic or fabric paints
◆ stencil brush

1. Use the purchased stencil or trace a motif onto stenciling paper (see *Stenciling Basics*, page 177) and cut it out with a craft knife, leaving the background intact.

2. Measure the stencil's width and mark the shade for evenly spaced designs. Then hold the stencil on the shade and gently stipple paint through the opening with the stencil brush. Carefully remove the stencil and let the paint dry.

PAINTING THE OUTLINE

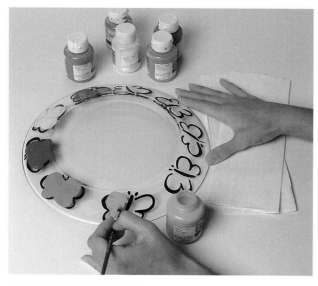

PAINTING THE WINGS

*H*ere's a wonderful way to blend craft and art to make the things you use distinctly personal.

Painting on Glass

Painting on the back of clear glass, as opposed to the surface, is often called reverse painting, but either way you are applying painted designs. Both translucent and opaque paints for glass are widely available in crafts stores; you just brush, stencil, or sponge them on and let them dry. Follow the manufacturer's directions for setting the paint. Note that the paints are permanent, but they should be placed on the back or outside of glassware where they won't come in contact with food.

Butterflies

YOU WILL NEED

- clear glassware such as a plate, bowl, vase, or butter dish, available in housewares stores
- paint for glass (we used Liquitex Glossies)
- no. 5 round paintbrush
- tracing paper
- adhesive tape

HOW TO MAKE IT

1. Trace one of the black butterfly outlines on page 132 a few times.

2. Cut out, arrange, and tape the patterns, facedown, on the front of the plate or bowl, or inside the vase or butter dish.

3. On the other side of the glass, paint the black lines and let the paint dry completely. (Practice applying paint smoothly on an old glass first. You can always wash off wet paint.)

4. Paint colored wings loosely as shown. Let the paint dry, then remove the patterns.

Other Ideas:
1. Dot with cotton balls or your fingertip.
2. Brush on random shapes.
3. Sponge-paint all over.
4. Cut and print sponges.

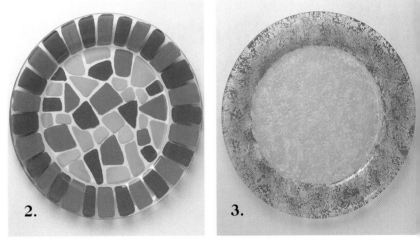

1.

2.

3.

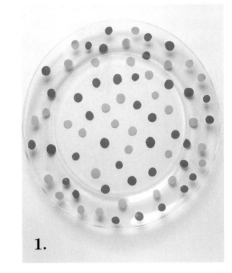

4.

Peach and Pear Cross-Stitch Pictures

❧ ❧ ❧

Show off your favorite hobby with style in hand-painted frames. If green is not for you, the charming fruit designs will look just as good in natural or stained-wood frames.

- 9 × 12-inch piece of 14-count ivory Aida cloth
- DMC Six-Strand Embroidery Floss, 1 skein each:
- *for the pear:* celadon 613, lime 907, pale lime 472, pale green 772, and pale citron 445
- *for the peach:* celadon 613, dark peach 3341, medium peach 353, pale peach 948, yellow 3078, pale lime 472, and pale green 772
- tapestry needle size 22
- 6- or 7-inch embroidery hoop
- sewing needle and any color thread
- small sharp scissors
- masking tape
- unfinished wooden frame for a 5 × 7-inch picture
- 5 × 7-inch acid-free barrier paper or board (from an art supply store) to back embroidery in frame
- optional: apple green acrylic paint to stain frame

HOW TO MAKE THEM

1. Place masking tape around the edges of the fabric to prevent raveling. Then fold the fabric in half lengthwise, then crosswise to crease the center lines. Baste along the lines with any color thread.

2. Cut an 18-inch length of floss from the skein to work (leave the paper on the skein to prevent tangling). Separate the floss to use 3 strands, and thread the needle. Center the fabric in the hoop with the weave straight.

3. *Cross-stitch:* Using 3 strands of floss, follow the charts (pages 136 and 137) in cross-stitch (see diagram, below), working each stitch over a square on the fabric. It can be helpful to mark the center lines on the charts and start your embroidery in the center. Each square on the chart represents one square on the fabric. To begin a thread, leave a 1-inch tail on the back and conceal it in the stitches as you work; to end off, run 1 inch of thread under stitches on the back and clip the end. *Be sure to cross each stitch in the same direction throughout.* Remove the hoop when not working.

3. *Lettering:* Work the lettering in backstitch (see diagram, below), using 3 strands of floss and working each stitch over a fabric square.

4. *Finishing:* Remove or cut off the tape. Place the embroidery facedown on a towel and iron it lightly from the back over a pressing cloth.

5. *Framing:* Remove the cardboard backing and glass from the frame. Paint the frame with water-thinned acrylic paint. Wipe off excess paint and let it dry. Place barrier paper, a thin padding if you like, then the embroidery on the front of the backing board, or place the embroidery over the acid-free board. Tape excess fabric to the back and secure the edges with the tape. Install the embroidery in the frame without glass.

CROSS STITCH

BACKSTITCH

pear

peach

These small pictures will be delightful wherever you hang them.

center

center

DMC COLORS

3078   472   772   3341   353   948   613

DMC COLORS

907 472 772 445 613

New Lamps from Old Teapots

❧ ❧ ❧

These lamps are sure to catch the eye anywhere. So if you find an old metal teapot at a flea market—think lamp.

- metal teapot or coffeepot (with a knob or ornament at the top that can be cut off or unscrewed)
- lampshade
- ⅜-inch-thick threaded lamp rod, cord, 4 hex nuts, plug, and a socket with switch (available separately or in kits from lamp departments and home centers)
- optional: a harp to hold the shade (buy the shade first in order to buy a harp the correct length)
- hacksaw
- drill with ⅜-inch bit
- rasp
- metal polish

HOW TO MAKE IT

1. Unscrew or saw off the knob or ornament at the top of the lid. Make sure the lid fits firmly in place.

2. Drill a hole for the rod through the center top of the lid. If the bottom of the pot is raised on legs or a rim, drill a hole through the bottom for the end of the rod. Cut an exit curve for the cord in the edge. If the bottom is not raised, drill an exit hole for the cord under the handle and plan to attach the rod to the lid only.

3. With the hacksaw, cut the rod long enough to extend about 2 inches above the top of the pot. Install the rod, screwing the nuts on the outside of the pot at each end or on the top and underside of the lid.

4. Run the cord up through the hole at the bottom of the pot and up through the rod. If you're using a harp, attach a nut, then the harp near the top of the rod. Separate the socket parts, and slip the bottom section onto the rod. Separate the two wires and slice off plastic at the ends to expose ½-inch wires. Attach one wire to each screw on the socket. Reassemble the socket at the top of the rod.

5. Attach the plug to the cord. Polish or clean the metal. Insert the bulb and add the lampshade. If the pot tends to tip, put a few rocks in the bottom to stabilize the lamp.

Old brass or silvery teapots make especially nice lamp bases because they reflect light from above. Polish them and electrify them with a kit from a hardware store.

Etched Glass

❧ ❧ ❧

Etched glass with its frosty and clear surfaces tends to fascinate us, whether on small objects or large glass storefronts. With a stencil and special cream, you can do your own professional quality etching on glasses, plates, and jars, but you must handle the materials with care.

YOU WILL NEED

- clean glass vase or perfume jar
- any window cleaner
- tracing paper
- transfer paper
- craft knife
- adhesive shelving vinyl (such as Con-Tact) to make the lace stencils shown, or pre-cut stencil of your choice
- masking tape
- Armour Etch Glass Etching Cream (from a crafts store)
- small round paintbrush
- *important: long-sleeved clothing, rubber gloves, and protective goggles*

HOW TO MAKE IT

1. Trace one of the lace half patterns, shown opposite, on folded tracing paper, placing the fold on the broken line. Trace the other half from your tracing to create the whole pattern. Or create your own design.

2. Place transfer paper facedown over the paper backing of the adhesive shelving material. Tape the pattern on top and trace the shaded areas onto the backing. Cut the stencil (see *Stenciling Basics*, page 177) through all the layers with the craft knife. Leave a border of vinyl around the outer edges. (If preferred, you can tape or glue the pattern directly onto the vinyl front and, without tracing, cut through the pattern and vinyl together.)

3. Clean the outside of the glass with the window cleaner to remove any grease. Peel off the paper backing of the cut stencil and smooth the stencil onto the glass. Apply tape over the outer edges.

4. *Put on your long-sleeved shirt, gloves, and goggles,* and protect your work surface with plastic or paper. *Then follow the manufacturer's directions precisely to apply etching cream* in the stencil spaces with the small brush. Let the cream dry for 5 minutes, as directed.

5. Finally wash off all traces of the cream with tap water and remove the stencil.

center

center

ETCHED GLASS PATTERNS

*O*rdinary glassware gets
a permanent doily design.

Wooden Bowls and Plates

❧ ❧ ❧

You can't eat off these, but they are fun to make and certainly useful and attractive filled with nuts in their shells, fruit, or laid out as underliners for glass plates. You simply paint plain wooden pieces from a crafts store.

HOW TO MAKE THEM

1. Stain wood with one coat of paint slightly thinned with water or apply two coats for solid color. Let the paint dry.

2. Decorate with simple repeated shapes. We made dots with a circle cut from a household sponge, but you could also use a cotton ball. Spatters are made by flicking paint from a flexible, long-bristled brush or by picking up paint on an old toothbrush and passing your finger over the bristles (be sure to practice first).

3. Apply a light coat of finish.

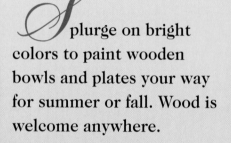

*S*plurge on bright colors to paint wooden bowls and plates your way for summer or fall. Wood is welcome anywhere.

CURTAINS

---✤---

Double Curtain

❧ ❧ ❧

Staple extra-long curtains to the back of a plywood valance and knot near the ends. The diagonal lines this creates may be all you need to add a little drama to a family room or small apartment. For a soft effect, try using two different-colored sheers.

- 12-inch-deep ¼-inch-thick plywood for the valance the width of the window frame
- two coordinating 45-inch-wide fabrics (about 1½ times the window width, and at least 24 inches longer than the window height to allow for hems and the knot)
- fabric 2 inches larger than the valance all around
- quilt batting the same size as the valance
- keyhole hangers and screws to install the valance
- power stapler
- matching thread or fusible tape for hems
- masking tape

1. Lay out the darker-color fabric for the valance wrong side up on a work surface. Center the batting, then the plywood on top. Pull the edges of the fabric over the plywood and staple them to the back. Start at the center of opposite sides, then staple the corners and edges, pulling the fabric firm and taut. Attach the keyhole hangers on each side and matching screws with protruding heads in the window frame.

2. If you want to add a lower border to one curtain, attach a 7-inch-wide (or any other size) band of the darker fabric to the lighter one. With right sides together, raw edges matching, pin, then stitch them together or fuse with web. Press the band down.

3. Turn under ¼ inch, then 1 inch around the curtain's edges and stitch or fuse them in place.

4. Gather the top of the lighter-color curtain by hand across the back of the valance about 3 inches above the lower edge; use masking tape to help set the gathers, then staple the fabric in place. Gather and staple the darker curtain over it.

5. Hang the valance from screws in the window molding. Then tie a knot at a different height near the bottom of each curtain.

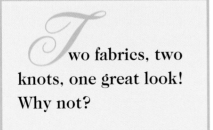

Two fabrics, two knots, one great look! Why not?

Gossamer Delight

❧ ❧ ❧

Sheers like this create a delicate atmosphere that invites tranquillity. Hang them in sunny rooms with cool green views.

YOU WILL NEED

- sheer tab-hung curtain long enough to fall below the windowsill when gathered near the bottom
- lightweight curtain pole or rod (paint it to match the ribbon if you like)
- 5 yards of ⅞-inch-wide satin ribbon
- artificial flowers for the tie and 2 for each curtain tab
- glue gun

HOW TO MAKE IT

1. Cut two strips of ribbon for loops to hold the curtain rod in front of the upper window frame. Thumbtack the ends over the frame near the corners, as in the photograph.

2. Slip the curtain onto the rod and hang it from the ribbon loops, or suspend it temporarily between two chairs while you add the flowers.

3. Cut a 27-inch length of ribbon for each tab. Glue a flower to both ends and tie the ribbon loosely around the tab with ends uneven. Hang the curtain from the window if you haven't already done so.

4. Gather the curtain gracefully below the middle with the remaining ribbon. Tuck and tie a nosegay or single flowers under the ribbon.

*H*ate to commit to hardware and unsightly nail holes? Hang a lightweight gossamer delight with ribbon loops.

Daisy Fresh Sheers

❧ ❧ ❧

Be sure to include the painted pegs at the top of the treatment to echo the daisy centers.

YOU WILL NEED

- pair of sheer tab-hung curtains
- Shaker-style peg rack to fit over the window frame
- tracing paper
- fine straight pins
- 1 yard of lightweight white piqué or other fabric
- ¼ yard yellow piqué fabric
- lightweight HeatnBond iron-on washable adhesive
- white and yellow latex or acrylic paint
- nails or screws and wall anchors to attach rack

HOW TO MAKE IT

1. Draw a pattern for a simple petal about 5½ inches long and a round flower center (trace a quarter). Decide how many flowers that are about 12 inches in diameter you want on the curtain and mark the placement by pinning tracings of the pattern to the curtain. The arrangement can be random or in rows of three, as shown.

2. Iron HeatnBond onto the back of the white and yellow fabrics, *following the manufacturer's instructions.* Trace as many centers and petals (five per flower) as you need on the paper backing. Cut out the shapes, then remove the backing. Pin the flower parts to the curtain front and iron them in place as directed, taking care not to scorch the curtain (work over a pressing cloth for safety).

3. Paint the rack white and the front of the pegs yellow. Install the rack above the window and hang the curtain tabs from the pegs. Two tabs can share a peg.

Dress up purchased sheers with subtle iron-on daisies and hang them from a Shaker-style peg rack.

Sponge-Printed Sheers

❦ ❦ ❦

The fabric triangle finishes the top of this treatment and helps to control light. It should fit across the rod when folded on the diagonal and hemmed with glue, tape, or stitching.

YOU WILL NEED

- sheer curtains
- square of fabric with a diagonal measurement at least 1 inch wider than the window frame
- fabric for painting
- fabric paint
- household sponge
- drop cloth
- rubber gloves
- coated plastic plate or disposable pie tin for the paint
- paper towels
- curtain rod
- thread, fabric glue, or fusible-web tape to hem the square

HOW TO MAKE IT

1. Cut the sponge into a 3-inch square (or any size rectangle or other shape you prefer).

2. Tape the curtain firmly to the drop cloth on a large table or the floor. The designs are printed at random, but if you prefer the security of pre-planning, make tracings of your pattern and pin or tape them in position on the curtain before painting. Pour a little fabric paint onto the plate, press the slightly damp sponge into the paint, and blot it on a paper towel or newspaper. Then remove any tracing and print on the curtain; you may get two prints from one application. Let the paint dry.

Tired of your plain store-bought sheers? Spark things up with an allover sponge print and the simplest valance—a fabric square folded over the top.

3. Finish the edges of the square valance fabric with ½-inch-wide glued, fused, or sewn hems. Hang the curtain from a rod at the top front of the window frame and fold the valance diagonally over the rod.

Tasseled Shade

❧ ❧ ❧

With cool floral fabric and handsome tassels, this is a rich but understated country look that complements rustic furniture and simple shapes and colors. It is a creative way to block out afternoon sun.

YOU WILL NEED

- fabric 1 inch wider and longer than the inside of the window frame
- tension curtain rod
- grommets and setting tool
- 5 yards rope or cord to fit the grommets
- two tassels
- thread or fusible-web tape for the hem

HOW TO MAKE IT

1. Turn under ½ inch all around the fabric and stitch or fuse it in place.

2. Fold and pin the fabric in half right side out with the ends together. Set an uneven number of grommets about 5 inches apart in matching positions along both sides 1 inch in from the edges and 2 inches from the top. The lowest grommet should be ½ inch from the bottom.

3. Cut the rope in half. Knot one end of one piece and pass it from the back through the top grommet on one side, then in and out through the grommets to the bottom. Let the end hang free for now. Repeat this on the opposite side.

4. Slip the rod through the top opening and hang the shade. Slide the fabric up to the height you want and knot the ends. Trim excess cord. Tie the tassels around the knots.

This shade is just as pretty seen from the outside when looking in.

Ribbon-Tied Towel

✦ ✦ ✦

With an inexpensive towel and a few yards of ribbon, the bathroom can become pretty and private. The rod pocket on this treatment is hot-glued, but if you don't have a glue gun, you can sew it instead.

YOU WILL NEED

- ◆ bath or hand towel
- ◆ three ribbons 5 times the length you want the shade to be (pairs will be cut from each ribbon)
- ◆ tension curtain rod
- ◆ buttons (optional)
- ◆ glue gun
- ◆ straight pins

HOW TO MAKE IT

1. Fold 3 inches at the top of the towel forward and glue or sew the edge in place. Glue or sew buttons along the front. Slip the curtain onto the rod and install the rod in the window.

2. Roll up the bottom of the towel to the desired height and secure it with pins. (Slightly less than halfway up the window is a good proportion and lets in light. The height cannot be easily adjusted once the ribbons are tied.) Cut the ribbons in half. Wrap each over the top, around the shade, and tie the ends together at different heights, as shown in the photograph. Fold the ends in half lengthwise and cut a slant from the outer corners to the fold to make dovetail ends.

*B*righten a bath with this terrific towel-and-ribbon curtain.

For a fairly sporty and lengthening effect, paint stripes on a bland matchstick blind, following the blind's own vertical binding. Top with a striped valance, varied with botanical cards.

Matchstick Blind

Blinds like these can bring order to a very busy room or add interest to a very simple decor. You'll get different effects with subtle stripes as in damask fabric or with strong ones as in awnings.

YOU WILL NEED

- matchstick blinds and hangers
- acrylic paint
- foam brush
- drop cloth

- ¼-inch foam-core board or ⅛-inch-thick hardboard to make a valance about 12 inches deep and the width of the window frame
- craft knife for foam core, saber saw for hardboard
- paint for background and stripes on hardboard or for stripes on foam core
- postcards or illustrations
- decoupage sealer/glue
- self-needling curtain hooks
- glue gun
- masking tape

HOW TO MAKE IT

1. Lay out the blind on the drop cloth and paint stripes on one side, working between every other pair of vertical bindings. When the paint is dry, turn the blind over and paint the other side. Install hooks in the window frame, near the top and hang the blind.

2. Trace a small plate or other curved object to make a pattern of two curves for the scalloped edge of the valance board. Mark the centers of the lower edge of the board and a scallop on the pattern. Matching centers to start, outline the pattern along the board, overlapping the previous marking with a pattern scallop as you move along the row. Cut in toward the points with the craft knife on foam core or saw on hardboard to cut the scallops.

3. If using hardboard, paint the background color and let the paint dry. On both hardboard and foam core, work out from the center to mask off the edge of vertical stripes about half the width of the stripes on the blind. Press the tape down firmly to obtain clean edges. Paint the stripes. Lift the tape carefully and let the paint dry.

4. Glue the illustrations to the valance *following the directions for your decoupage sealer/glue.*

5. The valance should cover the top of the window frame when hung over the blind with the self-needling hooks. Mark where the top of the hooks should fall on the back and hot-glue them evenly spaced to the valance. Then slip the hooks over the blind.

GARDEN THINGS

Patinaed Planter

If you can cut wood (or have straight pieces cut at a lumberyard), you can put this planter together with glue and screws. The patina is brushed on special coatings from a set you'll find in a crafts or paint store. Add creosote to the legs before decorating if you're going to place the planter on the lawn or in a garden where the ground may be damp.

SIZE

Exterior: 14½ inches square × 15 inches high; *interior:* 11¼-inch cube

YOU WILL NEED

- 5 feet of 1 × 12 pine for the box (see cutting, step 1)
- four 13¼-inch lengths of 2 × 2 pine for the corner posts/legs
- 4 feet of scallop-and-point ⅛-inch-thick molding
- four 1½-inch-long wooden finials
- patina coating set
- stiff bristle brush or sponge
- wood glue
- wood putty
- 2¼-inch galvanized flat-head screws
- ¾-inch brads
- white water-base primer
- paintbrushes
- drill with assorted bits
- matte polyurethane finish
- sandpaper
- masking tape
- saw

HOW TO MAKE IT

1. Cut the 1 × 12 lumber into five squares the same length as the board width. One square will be the box bottom, the others are the sides.

2. Glue and screw the box sides against the bottom, flush on the underside. (Predrill pilot holes with a countersink bit or drill holes narrower than the screw shank; then with a larger bit, drill space at the top to countersink the head.)

3. Drill five evenly spaced ⅜-inch-diameter holes into the bottom for drainage.

4. Mark the 13¼-inch corner posts 1 inch from one end for legs to extend below the box bottom. Prop the box level on 1-inch-high stacked wood, leaving the corners free. Glue the posts, with legs touching the ground, into the corners; clamp or tape the posts until the glue sets. Predrill holes for two countersunk screws (one each near top and bottom) through each post into the edges of the box sides. Insert the screws. Fill the tops with putty.

5. Cut four lengths of scallop (with a point centered) molding to fit between the posts. Glue and tack the molding to the outside of the box ¼ inch below the top.

6. Drill a hole in the center top of each post for the finial peg; apply glue to the pegs and glue the finials in place.

7. Sand the box lightly, rounding the edges. Brush on primer and let it dry.

8. Apply the patina *following the manufacturer's instructions.* When the patina is dry, apply two coats of clear finish.

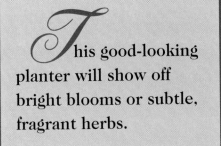

*T*his good-looking planter will show off bright blooms or subtle, fragrant herbs.

House Mailbox

✧ ✧ ✧

Bring the old mailbox inside to work, or start with a brand-new one. Let the woodworker in the family build the house. Then paint it and add the flowers.

YOU WILL NEED

- a standard 19-inch-long metal mailbox
- 1 × 8 pine lumber: one each 23 × 7⅛ inches and 23 × 6⅜ inches for the roof, and three 20½ inches for the sides and flowerpot shelf

- 4 inches of 2 × 4 lumber for the chimney
- 21 feet of 1⅛ × ¼-inch lattice strips for spacers and pickets
- board for underside to mount the mailbox
- 1-inch galvanized screws with nuts to mount mailbox through holes in the box
- four 1½-inch galvanized wood screws to attach house sides
- 1-inch and 2-inch finishing nails
- three 2-inch corner braces with ¾-inch wood screws to attach the shelf
- wood glue
- white primer
- red, black, yellow, blue, and green house and trim stain or exterior paint
- 1- and 2-inch foam brushes
- small round brush

- sandpaper
- drawing compass
- drill with ⅛-inch bit
- three 4-inch-diameter flowerpots
- saber saw

1. *Cutting:* Following the Assembly Diagram, below, glue and nail the 23-inch boards with the edge of the narrow one butted against the face of the wider one to form the roof peak. Cut two lattice strips 7¼-inch long as spacers between the wood sides and the mailbox to allow the door to open. Glue and nail a spacer across the inner face of each side board, 2½ inches in from the front edge. Cut one end of the chimney block at a 45-degree angle. Remove the flag plate and the flag from the mailbox. Following the diagram, draw and cut evenly spaced 3¾-inch-diameter holes in the remaining 20½-inch board for the pot shelf.

2. *Painting:* Sand the wood edges. Prime the roof, then paint it red. Paint the house sides and chimney yellow and the shelf green, letting each coat dry. Prime and paint the remaining lattice strips white to cut later for the fence.

3. *Side Assembly:* Hold the sides on the box, flush with the lower edge and extending 1 inch beyond the front. Mark the position of two existing mounting holes near the ends of each piece. Drill pilot holes for screws into the sides. Screw the mounting board under the mailbox and the house sides in place.

Chimney and Roof Assembly: Screw the flag to the chimney. Glue and nail the chimney to the roof. Bevel the outer top of the house sides with sandpaper. Glue and nail the roof to the top of the sides, allowing a 1¼-inch overhang at the front and back. *Shelf:* Install the pot shelf at the side with three evenly spaced braces. *Fence:* From the lattice, cut two 20½-inch and four 7½-inch strips for the rails. Cut twenty-five 4½-inch pickets. Cut a ½-inch-deep centered point at the top of each one. Attach the pickets evenly spaced and extending ½ inch below to the lower rails with glue and brads. With glue and 1-inch finishing nails, attach the upper rails to the edge of the shelf and pickets to the upper rail, leaving 1 inch between upper and lower rails.

4. *Finishing:* Prime and paint the top edge of the pickets and the nailheads. With the 1-inch brush, paint blue windowpanes on the house sides 3 inches from the ends. With black paint and the round brush outline shingles on the roof. Install the mailbox on its post, and place potted plants into the holes on the shelf.

mount flag to chimney

nail

45° angle

nail

6⅝"

1¼" overhang front and back

7⅛"

spacer

side

1½" screw

shelf

2½"

bevel

front

2"

1"

3¾"

2" braces

bottom strip

½"

1"

1"

HOUSE MAILBOX

Garden Tote

❧ ❧ ❧

This practical tote is made from a paint bucket and a strip of fabric that you pleat into pockets and attach with a hook and loop fastener. Only basic sewing skills are required.

YOU WILL NEED

- 2-gallon plastic paint or utility bucket with a handle and fairly straight sides
- medium-weight fabric 10 × 31 inches for backing (or 2 inches wider than the bucket circumference below the handle)
- medium-weight fabric 6 × 36 inches for the pocket panel (gingham with ⅜-inch checks is helpful when measuring pleats for the pockets)
- ¾-inch-wide Velcro Brand Hook and Loop Fastener Tape to fit around the bucket
- contact cement or Velcro glue

HOW TO MAKE IT

1. Separate the Velcro strip into hook and loop halves and glue the hook half around the bucket under the handle. On the upper long edge of the *backing fabric*, press 1 inch to the wrong side. Open the fabric flat. Stitch the loop half of the Velcro to the right side of the fabric flap above the crease. Refold the flap to the back with the Velcro facing out; topstitch ⅝ inch from the folded edge.

2. Fold under ¼ inch twice at the upper long edge of the *pocket fabric;* pin, topstitch, and press the edge.

3. Start about 3 inches from one end of the pocket fabric and fold a ⅜-inch pleat on the front toward the left, using the checks as a guide if possible (see the Folding Pockets diagram, right). Then measure 3⅜ inches from the outer fold toward the right for a pocket (9 gingham squares)

and pin a ⅜-inch pleat toward the right. Skip a 1½-inch space from the outer fold (4 squares) and pleat another pocket as before. Continue along the strip until you have 5 pockets and four 1½-inch spaces (do not trim excess fabric). Baste and press the pleats.

4. Now pin the right side of the pocket strip to the wrong side of the backing, 3 inches below the top of the backing, with the ginghams aligned if possible. Measure the length from the top of the Velcro to the bottom of the bucket; measure the same length from the top of the fabrics. Stitch across at this point for the bottom of the pockets. Trim the seam allowance to ½ inch. Turn the pockets to the right side. Press.

5. Pin and topstitch each side of the pockets to the backing, leaving the pleats free.

6. Press the two Velcro strips together to hang the backing on the bucket. Mark the fabric where the sides meet. Add ¾ inch to each edge. Remove the fabric from the bucket. Fold under ⅜ inch twice on the raw edges and topstitch along the folds. Press and rehang the fabric. Then tack the opening firmly closed at the center and bottom.

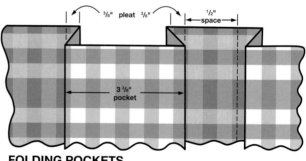

FOLDING POCKETS

*T*his bucket of blooms can also hold bulbs, prunings, stakes, seedlings, and more. And its clever pocketed apron takes care of the small stuff.

The handiest place to park small garden tools is in the garden, of course. A painted metal mailbox is a great weatherproof spot and very pretty to boot.

Mailbox Toolshed

❧ ❧ ❧

You don't have to go to all the trouble of setting a post for this mini shed. Just place it on top of a large flowerpot or an upturned log. And it's a nice way to recycle an old mailbox or refresh the one at the curb. The flowers are easy to make from one basic shape.

YOU WILL NEED

- a mailbox
- white primer for metal
- acrylic paints in yellow-green, medium green, white, yellow, periwinkle, brown, and dark pink
- 2-inch-wide flat paintbrush
- round paintbrush size 5 or 6
- a natural sponge or piece torn from a cellulose household sponge
- acrylic gloss spray finish
- sandpaper
- transfer paper

HOW TO MAKE IT

1. Prime the mailbox with the door open (if it's an old one, sand the surface first). Move the door while the primer dries to prevent sticking.

2. Paint the box with two coats of pale green (mix the green with yellow to brighten the color), letting each coat dry.

3. Sponge on medium green paint in irregular patches for a dappled appearance. Let the paint dry.

4. Plan groups of white daisies, blue forget-me-nots, pink asters, and yellow black-eyed Susans, or whatever flowers you like on paper. Indicate the placement of flowers on the box by taping on paper designs or using the transfer paper. Note that each flower shown is made the same way in different sizes. Make a circle and let

it dry; paint oval petals radiating around it. One basic oval shape can create a wide variety of flowers. To paint petals, place the round brush tip next to the flower center. Drag it outward, applying pressure to widen the shape. Then ease up to form a thinner tip. Vary the size and number of petals for different flowers (see petal diagrams and sizes, below) as follows:

Daisy: A dime-size yellow center and white petals.

Black-eyed Susan: Small dark brown center; bright yellow petals that are larger than the daisy's.

Aster: Small yellow-green center with many small petals in pinks and purples on branching stem; the aster should be smaller than the daisy.

Forget-me-not: Tiny pale yellow center; 5 small, rounder petals in blues.

5. Paint medium green stems connecting sprays of the same flowers with a round brush.

6. Finally, spray on two light coats of finish, letting each coat dry.

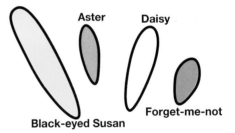

Petal sizes and shapes

Flowerpot Totem

~~~~~~~ ❧ ❧ ❧ ~~~~~~~

Accents at the end of lanes, tucked away, or right in the middle seem to protect the garden like ancient gargoyles. This totem can be conjured up from plastic flowerpots and wood scraps as a jolly guardian for your garden.

YOU WILL NEED

♦ 4 graduated-size lightweight plastic flowerpots: 1 each about 12 inches wide × 8 inches high, 10 inches wide × 7 inches high, 8 inches wide × 7 inches high, and 4 inches wide × 3½ inches high
♦ 23-inch-long 2 × 4 lumber
♦ scrap ¾-inch-thick wood
♦ 20-inch armature wire
♦ 22 each 1-inch drywall screws and ⅜-inch washers

*I*t's a butterfly, it's a turtle, it's a rabbit! It's all of them, plus a friendly frog for them to perch on—all made out of flowerpots

- white spray or brush-on primer
- acrylic paints (Delta Ceramcoat Spring Green, Luscious Lemon, White, Black, Pink Parfait, Apple Green, Wedgwood Blue, Blue Lagoon, and Royal Fuchsia)
- tracing paper
- transfer paper
- staple gun
- clear polyurethane or exterior acrylic finish
- wire snips
- tacky glue
- saw
- drill
- craft knife

1. Stack the pots upside down. Trim the 2 × 4 for the central post to the same height. Then unstack the pots. Trace the end of the post on the center bottom of the three largest pots, draw an X from corner to corner of the traced rectangle. Cut the X with a craft knife to form an opening for the post.

2. Trace the animal patterns, pages 164–166, and transfer the outer lines to wood using the transfer paper or by cutting out the patterns and tracing around the edge. Cut out the shapes with the saber saw (see *Making Wooden Cutouts*, page 176).

3. Prime the pots and wood shapes. Transfer any details, as on the butterfly wing, to the shapes with transfer paper. Then paint the pots and shapes, following the photograph and the patterns.

4. Drill holes for 2 screws through the pots into the shapes through the inside, aligning the parts so that all face forward when the pots are stacked on the post. Screw the pieces on, adding a washer under each screw.

5. Slip the 2 × 4 up through the pots one by one, stapling the flaps of the X cut to it as you go (see the diagram, below).

6. Drill holes for two antennae, the same width as the armature wire, into the top of the butterfly and the end of the post. Cut the armature wire in half with wire snips, curl the tips with pliers, and glue the straight ends into the holes.

7. Apply the clear finish, *following the manufacturer's directions*.

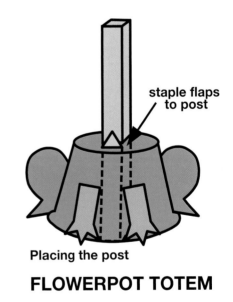

staple flaps to post

Placing the post

FLOWERPOT TOTEM

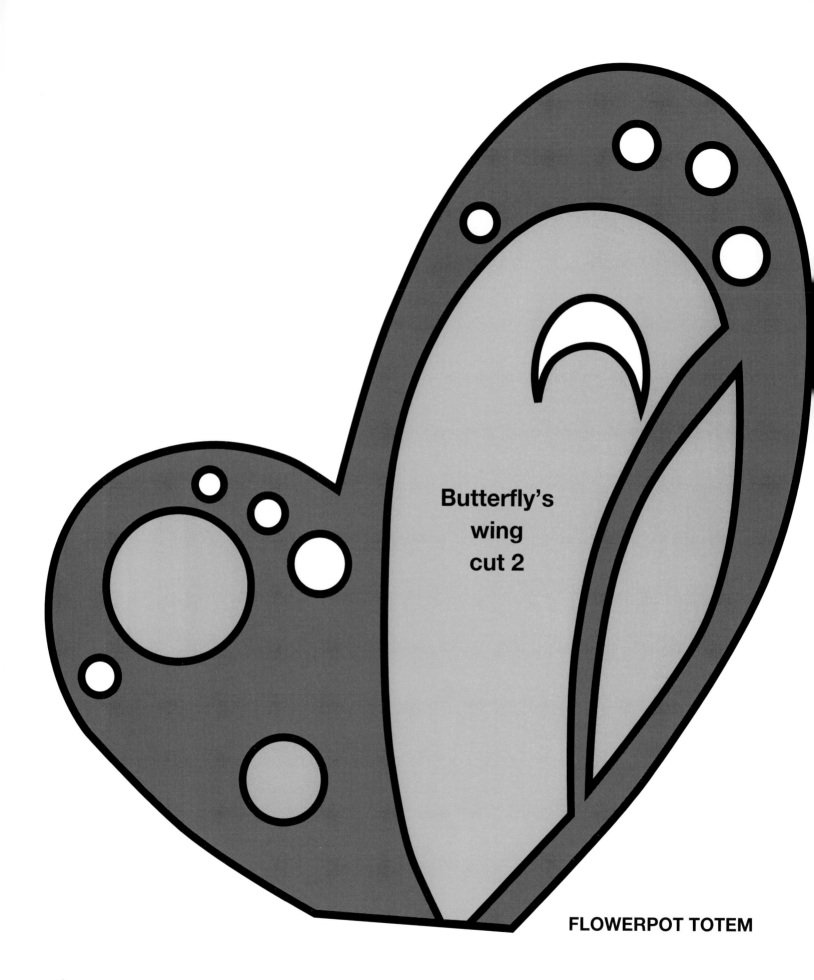

**Butterfly's
wing
cut 2**

FLOWERPOT TOTEM

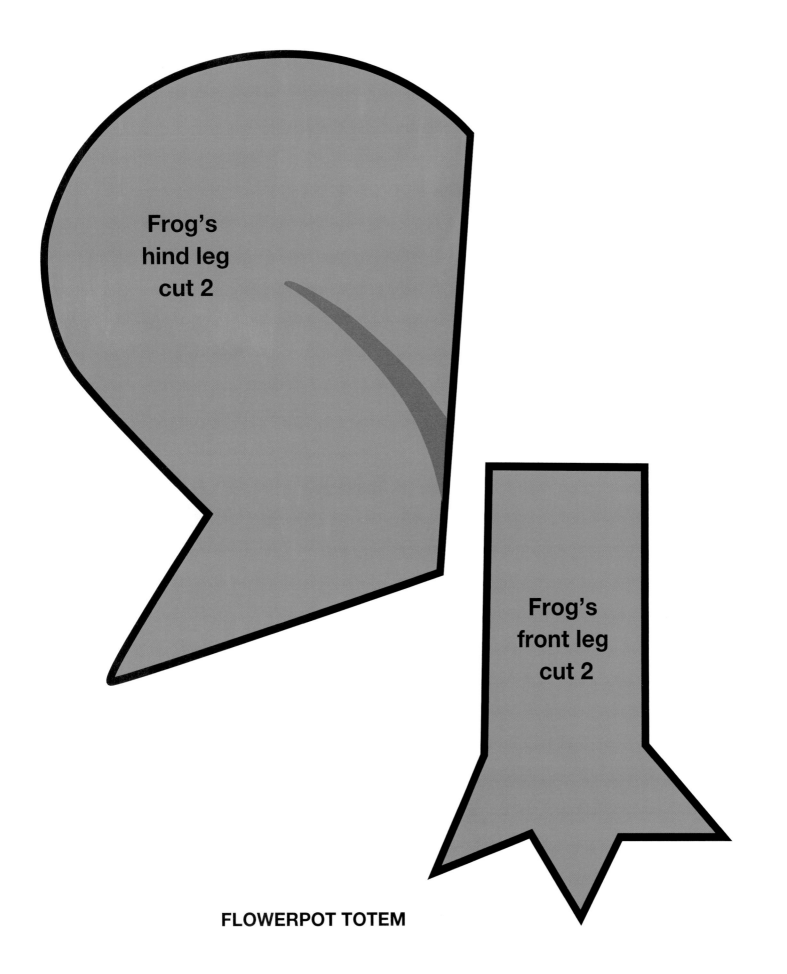

FLOWERPOT TOTEM

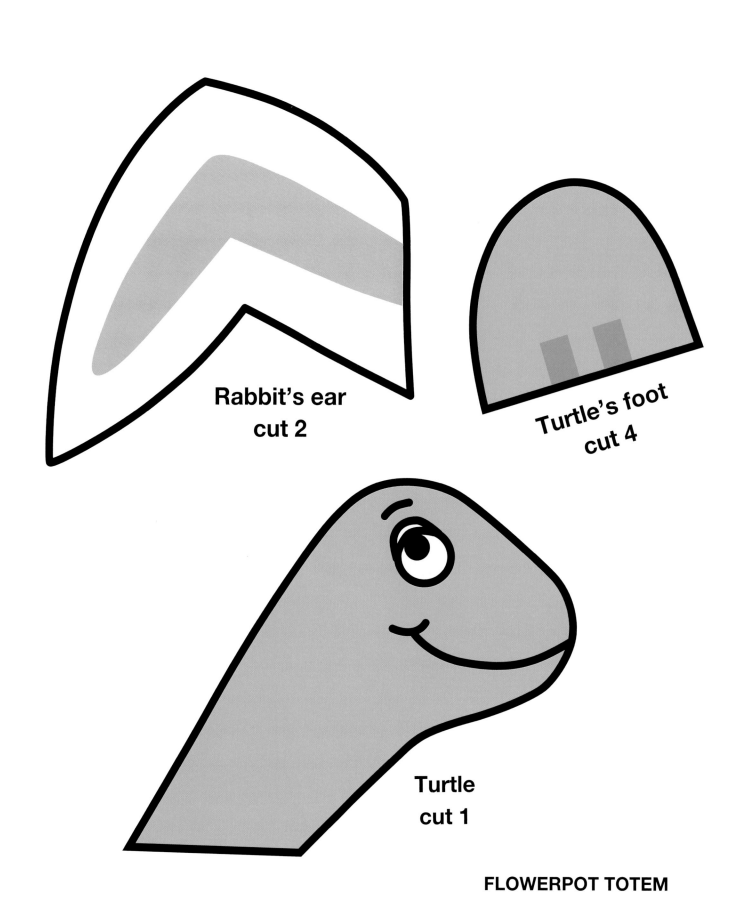

Rabbit's ear
cut 2

Turtle's foot
cut 4

Turtle
cut 1

FLOWERPOT TOTEM

Stenciled Watering Can

❧ ❧ ❧

Pretty tools for specific tasks can make ordinary chores a joy. So give a metal can a coat of paint, a crackle finish for a different texture and a bouquet of stenciled flowers. Save it to sprinkle the most delicate plants and herbs.

YOU WILL NEED

- galvanized metal watering can
- white primer for metal
- Driftwood Faux Crackle Finish Kit by Plaid Enterprises (from a crafts store)
- a flower stencil (Adele Bishop Cornflowers #87312)
- green acrylic paint for the spout
- acrylic or stencil paints for the flowers
- 1-inch flat paintbrush
- stencil brush
- masking tape
- plastic-coated plate or pie plate for paint
- acrylic gloss spray finish

HOW TO MAKE IT

1. Brush primer on the can, spout, and metal section of the handle and let it dry.

2. Apply crackle finish *as directed by the manufacturer* only to the can, not to the spout. Paint the spout green and the handle any color you wish.

3. When the paint is dry, tape the stencil to one side of the can. (Also tape over any parts of the stencil you don't want to use.) Pour a little paint onto the plate, dip the stencil brush into the paint, and swirl it on the plate or paper to even out the color on the bristles. Then stipple the paint onto the can through the stencil holes,

Stenciled flowers and crackled paint turn an ordinary watering can into a year-round beauty. In winter, bring it indoors to use as a vase.

working in from the edges and leaving lighter areas in the center to add highlights. Remove the stencil carefully and let the paint dry. Touch up the color with a brush if necessary.

4. Finally, spray on two light coats of finish, letting each coat dry.

Garden Guy

❧ ❧ ❧

Lightweight flowerpots are strung together with wire, assembled to form a figure and trimmed with moss. The top can be planted with live or artificial greens.

YOU WILL NEED

- plastic terra-cotta–colored flowerpots with several drainage holes around the bottom edge: sixteen 4 inch wide × 3½ inch high for arms and legs, two 8 × about 8 inches for the body, and one 6 inches wide × 5 inches tall for the head
- 6 yards of galvanized 14-gauge wire
- dried mosses
- wire cutters
- drill
- pliers
- glue gun
- plants and soil or artificial plants and florist's foam to fill the head

HOW TO MAKE IT

1. Drill holes about 1½ inches from the bottom and 7 inches apart in one large pot for the legs.

2. Run half the length of an 80-inch wire through the pot from drilled hole to drilled hole. On each end, string a leg of two small pots rim to rim and two more stacked inside each other.

3. Thread wire up through opposite holes in the pots and twist it around itself at the "hip" joints, using pliers.

4. Insert two 36-inch wires for shoulders down through two holes (leave one empty hole between them) on one side of a pot for the upper body or "chest," and up through two holes on the opposite edge, leaving ends at each side for arms. Twist the wire together at the shoulders.

5. Bend about a 45-inch wire in half and run the ends up through opposite holes on the lower body pot and through the inside of the "chest" pot (between the arm wires). Draw the lower and upper body pots together and twist the wires together at the top. Glue the body pots together at the waist.

6. Insert the arm wires down through opposite holes in four small pots, stacked and curved as in the photograph, and twist the ends together.

7. Wire the bottom of the head pot to the shoulder and body wires at the top.

8. Glue moss into the joints. Fill the head pot with soil and live plants, or use plastic foam and artificial plants.

This flowerpot fellow is an eye-catching accent that will look especially impressive in perennial country beds or ivy-covered city yards. Add moss and greens for character and charm.

Boy on a Swing

❧ ❧ ❧

When you've done everything else—the ironing, the cleaning, the gardening—and you have nothing else to do inside or out, add this little fellow of cut and painted wood to a tree limb in the backyard.

YOU WILL NEED

- pine lumber or ¾-inch exterior plywood, 11¼ × 20 inches
- 14-inch 2 × 4 or other 3½-inch-wide wood for the swing seat
- eight 2-inch nails
- two 2½-inch wood screws
- ¼-inch-thick sisal twine or other rope for hanging the swing
- white primer
- transfer paper

- acrylic paints (Delta Ceramcoat White, Cayenne, Flesh, Napthol Crimson, Napthol Red, Ocean Blue, Opaque Yellow, and Spring Green)
- black paint pen marker
- clear polyurethane or exterior finish
- paintbrushes
- sandpaper
- saber saw
- drill
- tacky glue

HOW TO MAKE IT

1. Enlarge the pattern (see *How to Enlarge Patterns*, page 174). Transfer the outlines to wood over the transfer paper and cut out the pieces with the saber saw. Sand the edges (fill plywood edges with wood putty if necessary).

2. Prime all sides of each wood piece. Let the primer dry.

3. Transfer the outlines for solid areas such as the pants, shirt, face, and cap, and paint two coats on the front and sides. When the paint is dry, paint the back of the clothes to correspond to the front. Let the paint dry.

4. Transfer the pattern outlines and paint the details such as hair, cap bill, shirt stripes, and knee patch over the undercolor. Draw the black lines with the marker. Lightly dab on pink cheeks with a cotton ball or paper towel. When the front is dry, continue the details on the back.

5. Drill a ⅜-inch-diameter hole for rope centered 1¾ inches from each end of the 2 × 4 seat.

6. Mark the placement of the boy centered ½ inch from the back on the swing seat. Drill pilot holes for 2 screws up through the seat in the marked area. Then glue and screw the boy's body in place.

7. Glue and attach the legs to the front of the seat with two nails each.

8. Cut two generous lengths of twine for hanging the swing. Tie a large knot in one end of each string and secure it with a drop of glue. Thread one strip each up through the holes in the seat and glue them over the front of the boy in hand position. Nail the hands to the arms, tilted to cover the twine as if holding it. Touch up the nailheads.

9. Brush on two coats of finish, letting each coat dry. Then tie the ropes to a branch on a tree.

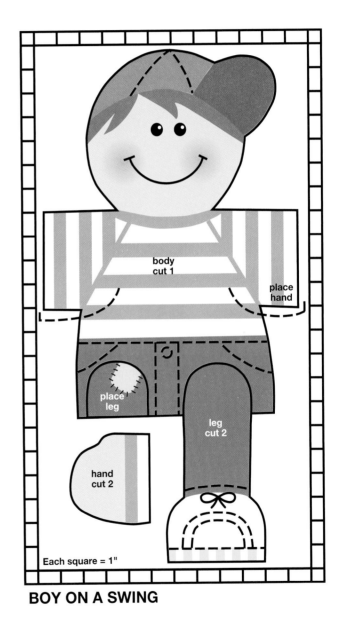

BOY ON A SWING

Crafts Terms

※ ※ ※

Acrylic paint: A water-base artist's paint available in crafts, art supply, and paint stores. Can be used opaque or thinned with water for stains and washes. It dries quickly. Use with synthetic brushes, and clean up with soap and water before the paint dries.

Backing or back of quilt: The outer layer of fabric on the back.

Batt or batting: A fabric of synthetic or cotton fibers in various thicknesses used inside quilts and quilted objects.

Binding: A strip of fabric that encloses and finishes the edges of a quilt.

Block: In quilting, an assembled square of fabric repeated in the design.

Clear finish: Any coating or varnish to protect painted and wood surfaces, such as acrylic crafts finishes and polyurethane. Use an exterior finish for outdoor projects.

Clip corners: Cut diagonally across the seam allowance on sewn corners to make them sharp when turned right side out.

Craft glue stick: White or clear glue in stick form (not to be confused with glue sticks for glue guns); excellent for gluing paper smoothly.

Craft knife: A knife with changeable fine, sharp, pointed blades, such as an X-Acto knife.

Decoupage: Decoration made from cut and pasted papers.

Decoupage sealer/glue: An adhesive especially made for sealing wood and gluing on decorative paper or fabric cutouts.

Dimensional paint: Crafts or fabric paint applied from a nozzle-tipped squeeze bottle to achieve a raised line.

Fabric paint: A flat or dimensional paint made especially to bond smoothly to fabric and that can be washed without fading.

Fish line: A clear nylon monofilament suitable for tying and stringing materials.

Flat paintbrush: Brush with a tip cut straight across; sometimes called a shader.

Foam brush: An inexpensive sponge brush, it can be used instead of a bristle brush for painting, applying glues and finishes. It can be washed for reuse before the medium dries or it can be discarded.

Foam-core board: Polystyrene foam sandwiched between two layers of cardboard.

Glue gun: An electrical, gun-shaped instrument with special glue in stick form that is applied hot and acts as an instant bond for bulky materials including wood. Use a low-temperature gun and sticks for fabric or foam projects.

Grain of fabric: The crosswise and lengthwise direction of the woven threads.

Graph paper: Paper with light-colored grids of various sizes. To enlarge patterns, buy paper large enough for your project with 1-inch lines clearly marked.

Masking tape: A tan or white removable adhesive paper tape sold in various widths.

Mitered corners: Corners that are cut or folded to meet at an angle, usually 45 degrees on a right-angle corner, as on quilts or moldings.

Patchwork: Fabric assembled from small pieces stitched together.

Pillow form: A soft, ready-made pillow shape to be covered.

Primer: A thin undercoat that seals the surface of wood before painting.

Removable tape: Any sticky-back temporary tape, such as drafting, masking, painter's, or clear plastic tape, designed for easy removal.

Right side of fabric: The outer face you want showing on the finished project.

Rotary cutter: A wheeled tool that makes cutting fabric, especially long straight pieces in multiples, easier and quicker.

Round paintbrush: A round artist's brush with bristles tapered to a point.

Seam allowance: The fabric between the seam and the cut edge on sewn pieces.

Slip stitch: A fairly invisible stitch for sewing a folded edge to another folded edge or flat fabric.

Sponge painting: Dabbing paint on with a slightly damp sea sponge or piece of cellulose household sponge to create a mottled surface.

Stencil: A template cut with openings for painting repeated designs.

Stencil brush: A round brush with stiff bristles and flat tip for stippling paint through stencils.

Synthetic brush: One made of synthetic rather than natural fibers.

Tacking stitch: A few small stitches over each other to attach fabric or small decorations.

Tacky glue: A thick white glue that dries clear, for adhering slightly bulky materials.

Template: A full-size pattern cut from cardboard, plastic, or other durable material for repeated use.

Topstitch: A line of stitching made on the right side of the fabric and intended to show.

Tracing paper: Paper you can see through for tracing. Use medium-weight paper for patterns.

Transfer paper: Paper, such as carbon paper, that will transfer marks from one sheet of paper to another paper or surface when under pressure.

White craft glue: A common, many purpose water-soluble white glue that dries clear.

Wrong side of fabric: The back of the fabric. On some woven fabrics the back is often hard to distinguish from the front. Looking at the selvage sometimes helps. Choose the back and mark it.

Crochet Abbreviations

CC—contrasting color

Ch—chain stitch

Dc—double crochet stitch

Dec—decrease

Hdc—half double crochet stitch

MC—main color

Right side—front of work when finished

Round—a circular or square row

Row—a straight row

Sc—single crochet stitch

Sp—space

St(s)—stitch(es)

Tr—treble crochet stitch

Wrong side—back of work when finished

Yo—yarn over hook

Asterisk*—work the instructions following * and repeat them as indicated

Parentheses ( )—repeat or work the inclosed instructions as indicated. At the end of rows, the number of stitches or groups you have made on the row is enclosed in parentheses.

Furniture Preparation

Remove any hardware and drawers before you begin (unless the design depends on having them installed). On some pieces you can cover the hardware with tape before painting. Lay the piece flat as needed to work easily and always protect the floor with a drop cloth or newspaper. Follow the manufacturer's directions for the use of commercial materials, and be sure to work in a well-ventilated area when required.

If an old piece is painted and you want to paint it again, wash and dry the surface thoroughly, but quickly, to keep water from getting into cracks and warping the wood. Fill any crevices with wood putty and let the putty dry. With sandpaper, smooth the putty, but roughen the paint to receive new paint. It's important to wipe off any sanding residue, preferably with a tack cloth, available in hardware stores.

If you want to stain the piece with a commercial stain or a thin coat of acrylic paint, you must work on raw wood. On an old piece, remove the finish completely using a commercial stripper. Then sand the surface, if it feels rough, with a block of fine (220-grit) sandpaper, following the grain. If the piece has spindles, use strips of sandpaper or a foam sanding block or a round sanding tool on a drill to work on curves. Wipe off the residue with a tack cloth.

On new, unfinished wood, sand the surface lightly if it feels rough and wipe it with the tack cloth before applying any finish.

Use synthetic brushes with acrylic paints. Inexpensive foam brushes are easy to use and can be discarded when you're finished; they just don't hold as much paint as bristle brushes.

How to Enlarge Patterns

Patterns that are larger than the pages of this book have to be enlarged on a photocopier or on graph paper.

To photocopy: Color patterns can be enlarged on black-and-white copiers as well as on color copiers. Enlarge successive copies of the pattern until the grid is the size required. For example, if the scale is each square = 1 inch, each grid square on the copy should be 1 inch. Very large patterns will have to be enlarged in sections. Enlarge each section to the required size, then match up the lines (trim excess paper if necessary) and tape the papers together.

To draw on a grid: This is the traditional method of making an enlargement to scale. With a pencil and ruler, draw a grid on the pattern by connecting the grid lines indicated on the edges. On graph paper or plain paper, draw the same grid, making each square the required size. In each square, copy the lines from the corresponding square of the pattern. If the pattern is complex, number each square on the pattern and your grid to help keep your place.

HOW TO TRANSFER PATTERNS

After you have made or traced full-size patterns, transfer them to your crafts materials using one of the following methods.

To use transfer paper: Transfer papers such as graphite paper, dressmaker's carbon, or multipurpose paper are available in crafts, fabric, and art supply stores. Use a transfer paper especially when there are many inner detail lines on the pattern. Place the transfer paper facedown over your material. Place the pattern face up on top and tape the edges in place with removable tape. Go over the pattern lines with a pencil or tracing wheel to transfer them. Remove the paper.

To transfer without transfer paper: *Pencil method:* This is an ages-old, basic method that is inexpensive and easy to do. With a soft, dark pencil, scribble lines on the back of the pattern. Pin or tape the pattern face up on your craft material and draw accurately and firmly over the lines. Remove the pattern. If the transferred lines are not distinct, clarify them with a pencil or marker. *Cutout method:* To transfer simple shapes such as quilt motifs, cut out the traced pattern on the outline. Pin or tape the pattern in place on your material and trace around the edge. If you will be making several copies (as for a quilt), cut the pattern from cardboard or a firm sheet of plastic to make a template that will hold its shape better than tracing paper will.

To transfer half patterns: Some of the patterns in this book are half patterns, with a broken line indicating the center of the shape. This is not just to save space; it ensures that both sides of the shape will be the same. *To transfer a half pattern to fabric:* Fold and pin the fabric in half, wrong side out. Pin the pattern firmly in place with the center line on the fold. Trace the outline and cut, or simply cut along the pattern edge, through both layers.

To make a whole pattern from a half pattern: After enlarging the pattern from the book, or when tracing a full-size half pattern from the book, fold tracing paper in half and place the fold on the center line of the pattern. Trace the outline on the top layer of the tracing paper. Cut out the pattern through both layers, leaving the fold uncut. Turn the folded tracing over and trace any details from the other side. Then open the pattern flat.

Making Wooden Cutouts

Make the pattern: Enlarge the pattern on paper or draw a grid with pencil and ruler or T-square to scale directly on the wood (see *How to Enlarge Patterns*, page 174). Include lines for details. If you're drawing the pattern directly on wood, make the lines fairly dark so they will show through the white primer when it dries. Or cut out the paper pattern and transfer the outline to the wood with transfer paper. Details can be applied later over the primer or paint.

Cut the wood: When sawing, wear safety goggles and a mask (available at lumberyards and paint and hardware stores) to protect your face from chips and sawdust. Clamp the wood firmly on a worktable with a C-clamp (place cardboard or wood under the clamp to prevent dents), with the part you're cutting extending over the edge. Cut out the shape with the required saw. To turn corners and navigate tight curves, cut excess wood from the edge to remove small sections at a time. When drilling holes all the way through, place scrap wood behind the piece you are drilling to keep the back of the wood from splitting and to protect the worktable.

Sand, prime, and paint the wood: Fill any large gaps in the plywood with wood putty. Let the putty dry, then sand the putty and the wood edges. Apply white primer to seal the wood (unless you are planning to apply color as a thin stain). The white background will also make the colors bright and clear when you paint. When the primer is dry, transfer detail lines from the paper pattern if you have not already done so. Brush on the paint with foam or bristle brushes, letting each color dry to the touch before painting the adjacent color. Lay down masking tape or painter's tape to guide straight lines, pressing the edges down firmly. Details, such as facial features, arm outline, and designs can be added over dry paint.

Quilting Basics

1. You'll find appropriate fabrics in most large fabric stores. Smaller specialty stores may offer a more extensive selection of coordinated patterns for quilters. It is important to prewash and iron cotton fabrics to be used in making quilts in warm water and mild soap to prevent uneven shrinking and running dye when the quilt is laundered. Wash dark colors separately. For very dark colors, you can add 2 tablespoons of vinegar to the rinse water to help prevent further running.

2. Cutting can be done most easily and accurately with a rotary cutter and mat unless the shape is irregular. They enable you to stack a few layers of fabric so you can cut several pieces at a time. To save time and improve accuracy, instead of cutting several small pieces, first cut a long strip the *width* of the small pieces. Then cut the long strip into the lengths you need.

3. To stitch seams, pin the fabric's right sides together with raw edges matching. Insert the pins at right angles to the edge so you can stitch over them. Stitch with a ¼-inch seam allowance (usually included in the cutting), or as directed, and carefully guide the edge of the fabric along the

¼-inch mark or required seam width on your machine. (Mark a guideline on tape at the right-hand side of the needle if your machine has no ¼-inch mark.) Press seam allowances toward the darker fabrics.

4. Use long basting stitches by hand or pins to hold the top, batting, and back together when assembling the quilt. Be sure to baste thoroughly from the center out to sides and corners to keep the fabrics smooth.

5. To stitch decorative quilt lines by machine,

roll the quilt up wrong side out to fit it under the machine arm. Secure the roll with pins, if necessary. Stitch with medium-length stitches and loosen the machine tension to accommodate thick fabric. To start and end, either backtack two stitches or stitch in place on zero setting. Pull threads to the back of the quilt, knot and clip to the fabric. If you prefer to quilt by hand, knot the thread and pull the end into the quilt between layers. Or run thread between layers by hand with a needle.

Stenciling Basics

Although you can purchase ready-made stencils, it's not hard to cut your own, and it's certainly worth it to do original work. You simply draw the shape on the stencil and cut it away to leave an opening. Paint is applied through the opening. The stencil material should be one that won't get soggy from the paint: waxed stencil paper, matte acetate sheets (.005 mm), plastic blanks, and other materials are available in art supply and crafts stores. Use one you can see through to make placing the stencil easier for painting.

To draw the stencil, lightly tape the stencil blank over your pattern and trace the design with a pencil or marker. Trace separate stencils for sections that will be different colors—for example, flower leaves. Include a few guidelines from the main design for positioning the details.

To cut, place the stencil on a hard, smooth surface, such as heavy glass, wood, or cardboard and cut out the shapes with a fine craft knife or stencil knife. Leave a border at least 1 inch wide around the edge. (To cut smooth curves, turn the stencil

instead of moving the knife.) Cut away marker outlines if they will come off on the paint. Small mistakes can be bandaged with clear tape.

To paint, lightly tape the stencil to the project. Mix enough color for the whole job; cover the paint when it is not in use. Then pour a little paint onto a plastic or foam plate, disposable pan, or palette. Use a dry stencil brush and dip the end of the bristles into the paint. Then blot and even the paint on the bristles by swirling or dabbing the brush on a bare spot on the plate or on paper. You need only a little paint at a time.

Working in from the edges, paint with an up-and-down, stippling motion, through the stencil openings. Lift off the stencil when the paint is semidry or dry. Leave it in place if you will be adding shading. Align any detail or second-color stencils over the dry first image and apply the paint as before.

To clean, wash paint off the stencil or let it dry hard before turning a stencil over to use the other side to paint a reversed image.

Where to Buy Crafts Materials

Large crafts and fabric chain stores have a dazzling array of supplies and materials. You will usually find everything you need for a project in one store—paints, fabrics, embroidery threads, dried flowers, paper, glue, clear finishes, and bottles, as well as materials you've never imagined. Art supply, variety, and paint stores have added crafts supplies to their inventories. Lumberyards and home centers are sources for wood, hardware, paints, and tools. Unfinished furniture is available in both crafts stores and special stores for unfinished wood pieces, where they may custom build as well. And don't forget local needlework and fabric stores, garden centers, and floral suppliers. If you haven't investigated these sources before, start by looking in the commercial pages of your phone book. And if you still cannot find specific supplies listed for a project—the exact yarn or paint, for example—substitute similar available materials.

INDEX

CREDITS

CRAFTS DESIGNERS
Yvonne Beecher: 135; Teresa Caruso: 38; Judith Hoffman Corwin: 78; Joanne Grossman: 64; Pat Henry: 47; Margot Hotchkiss: 96, 128; Jacqueline Jewitt: 69, 75; Dale Joe and Jack Champlin: 28; Jann Johnson: 141, 159; Richard Kollath: 84, 142; Kollath-McCann Creative Services: 2, 11, 32, 33, 112, 124, 130, 169; Michael Lane: 17; Ingrid Leess: 90, 114, 117, 144, 146, 147, 148, 149, 150, 151; Ellen Liberles: 71; Karin Lidbeck: 12, 87, 160, 167; Kathi Malarchuk: 6; Lina Morielli: 50; Julia Morrill: 82; Cindy Taylor Oates: 138; Brent Pallas: 8, 15, 20, 24, 26, 31, 35, 93, 107, 116, 118, 121, 122, 127, 129, 132, 133, 154, 156, 162, 170; Philene Rivera: 23; Mimi Shimmin: 55, 59, 62, 102, 110; Jim Williams: 44, 98, 107

PHOTOGRAPHERS
Alban Christ: 98, 156; Bill Holt: 8, 11, 23, 24, 32, 78, 80, 87, 107, 112, 121, 122, 130, 138, 154; Len LaGrua: 42, 56, 106, 132, 133; Kit Latham: 151, 162; Bruce McCandless: 71; Jeff McNamara: 15, 33, 90, 114, 117, 129, 141, 144, 146, 147, 148, 149, 150; Tom McWilliam: 2, 6, 20, 31, 41, 44, 55, 62, 75, 124, 127, 159, 160, 167, 169, 170; Douglas Morrill: 83; Bradley Olman: 29, 35, 116, 128; Luciana Pampalone: 26, 82, 96, 102, 135; Joe Polillio: 47, 64, 107, 110, 142; Steven Randazzo: 28; William Seitz: 50; William P. Steele: 84, 118; Bill Stites: 17; Marcus Tullis: 69, 93; Judith Watts: 12